CALLED TO RISE

CALLED
TO RISE

A LIFE IN
FAITHFUL SERVICE
TO THE COMMUNITY
THAT MADE ME

DAVID O.
BROWN

WITH
MICHELLE BURFORD

BALLANTINE BOOKS

NEW YORK

Copyright © 2017 by David O. Brown

Published in the United States by Ballantine Books,
an imprint of Random House,
a division of Penguin Random House LLC, New York.

BALLANTINE and the HOUSE colophon are registered
trademarks of Penguin Random House LLC.

Hardback ISBN 978-1-5247-9654-9

Ebook ISBN 978-1-5247-9655-6

Printed in the United States of America on acid-free paper

randomhousebooks.com

246897531

First Edition

Title-page photo: © 2017 The Dallas Morning News, Inc./Tom Fox

Book design by Barbara M. Bachman

To my mother, Norma Jean—

Thank you for sacrificing so much
to give me all that matters.

Your strength gives me strength
every single day.

———

To the fallen heroes of July 7, 2016—

Your extraordinary courage will forever live on

in the memories of those you served.

———

To my wife, Cedonia—

I love you.

CONTENTS

———

CALLED TO RISE

CHAPTER 1

THE CALLING

—

I NEVER SET OUT TO BE A COP. BUT AFTER RETURNING TO MY hometown during the summer after my sophomore year of college, I was so terrified by what I witnessed that it awakened in me a potent determination to intervene.

The year was 1982. What was happening in my Dallas neighborhood of Oak Cliff was happening in communities all across the country: A crack epidemic, one more destructive than any drug pandemic before it, was devastating America's inner cities in particular. Crack, a cheap form of cocaine that dealers turned into a smokable crystallized solid, could be measured out in smaller and more affordable quantities to peddle to the poor. But coke's less expensive derivative had an even stronger power to hold users in its grip. Many who used were often willing to do whatever it took to get their next fix—even steal or kill. Many who sold found themselves engaged in turf wars to protect their sales territory. The homicide rate among black men spiked significantly after crack came on the scene. Gun violence became a way of life, for those engaged in the trade and for residents who lived in close proximity to drug houses. Before I'd left my hometown to enroll at the University of Texas at Austin, I didn't know a single person who'd been killed. But that summer two years later, a kid on my block was fatally shot in the cross fire of a deal gone sour.

Even after I returned to college that fall to begin my junior year, my head and heart stayed back in Oak Cliff. All semester I'd call home frequently to check on my beloved mother and my younger brother, Kelvin, who was living with her. Every morning and evening in the dark, amid this Armageddon, my mother had to navigate her way to the bus stop for work. I feared so deeply for her that I'd often awaken in the middle of night and be unable to get back to sleep. I couldn't concentrate on my course work. "Pay close attention to your surroundings." She responded the way she had for all my childhood. "I'm just trusting in the Lord," she said. "He will protect me." Though I prayed she was right, I felt Him calling me to do something.

For me, that desire was intensely personal. Oak Cliff was the community that had made me. It's where I'd shot hoops and formed lifelong friends, the place where I'd found my feet and became grounded in my faith. It's where three generations of my family had lived and worked and hoped for better, where my mother had reared three sons on only a secretary's salary and a prayer. I couldn't just stand by and watch my family in danger and my hometown destroyed. I had to step up. The way I saw it, the fools who were selling crack in the very neighborhood that had produced us needed to be locked away. They were killing us. Though I soldiered on through my course work, I'd already made a decision: I would leave school and join the Dallas Police Department.

The plague of crack was the main reason I decided to join the force, but there was something else pulling me back to Dallas and into a life of adult responsibility. During my freshman year, I'd started seriously dating a girl I'd met in high school, and in 1982, we got married. A few months later I discovered we were expecting. So the following spring, once my junior year was complete, we moved back to Oak Cliff and rented a small apartment.

Did it bother me to leave college with one year to go? It did. I had this nagging sense of a task undone, a goal not met. I'd seen higher education as a passageway out of poverty, a chance for me to make something of myself. In pursuit of that goal, I'd invested countless hours in the library, poring over my textbooks. I'd worked constantly to keep my grades up so I could earn a scholarship. And once I'd enrolled in the university, I'd flourished academically and socially and formed a new circle of friends. By walking away, I'd be sacrificing all of that, and though it was for a cause I felt I couldn't deny, I still wished I could complete my studies. So I put a plan in place: If I was accepted onto the force, I would transfer to a school in the University of Texas system in Dallas and continue my course work on the side.

In June 1983, my precious son, David Junior—or D.J., as I affectionately call him—was born. His tiny body nearly fit in my cupped palms. From the moment I first held him, my desire was to give him everything I didn't have as a child, as well as to pass on the strong wisdom and faith my family had instilled in me. Even before I cradled him for the first time, with my Afro as full and thick as the Dallas humidity, I loved him unconditionally. Becoming a parent has the ability to alter the very way you love, and so it did for me. I cherished my son not because of anything he would ever be able to offer to me but simply because he existed. Nothing he could do would change that. On the day he was born, I put on the mantle of fatherhood, shoulders lifted and heart full, ready to nurture and protect and, above all else, provide. That is what being a good father meant to me—providing.

As I settled into a routine of diaper changing and bottle feeding, I made plans to apply to the force. My own father didn't like the idea. "Why do you want to be a cop?" he asked me. "There are so many great things you could do with your life. Cops mistreat people in the community."

I understood my dad's perspective. He'd come of age at a time when police officers had been the ones to enforce the indignities of segregation; that experience had not only scarred him, it had shaped his worldview. It was only out of concern for me that he voiced his dissent. I'm sure my mother was just as worried, but she didn't try to dissuade me. "You just be careful, son," is all she told me. She could probably sense that I was immovable in my resolve.

On a clear morning that July, I left my one-month-old son at home and departed for the municipal building at 106 South Harwood Street, the old police headquarters where Lee Harvey Oswald had been arrested and jailed after he assassinated President John F. Kennedy. There, on the fourth floor, I asked for an application. The secretary, a black woman in her late thirties, looked me up and down. "You aren't likely to be hired," she told me. I suspected she said that because I still looked and acted like the inner-city kid I was proud to be, but I didn't care what she thought. "I'm going to be a police officer," I snapped back. She handed me the form. I stood there and filled it out and returned it to her the second I was finished. I left the building that day certain of only one thing: I wouldn't take no for an answer.

David, my former college roommate, called me soon after I'd applied. I told him I wasn't planning to return to college in the fall because I was entering the force.

"How much do they pay?" he asked. I told him the starting salary was just under twenty thousand dollars.

"Well, I'm moving to Seattle after my senior year," he told me.

"What's in Seattle?" I asked.

"A company called Microsoft is hiring," he told me. At UT Austin, he'd already proven to be a mathematics and computer whiz. "Why don't you move up there with me?"

"Nah, man," I told him. "I've gotta stay here in Oak Cliff."

"Why do you want to be a police officer?"

"Because they're hiring," I told him. "I've got a baby who needs diapers and formula." I'm not sure why I gave him only half of the story. Maybe I assumed he wouldn't understand. But my desire to become a police officer wasn't just a practical solution to my young family's financial needs; there were plenty of jobs out there, plenty of ways to earn a living. The fact is, I had never felt more drawn in a particular direction. The magnetic pull was strong and unyielding. I didn't just *want* to return to Oak Cliff to take up law enforcement; I felt I *needed* to go back there. Fifteen years later, David, who indeed joined Microsoft, cashed out his stock and retired. That was his path. I had to follow my own.

A few weeks after I applied, when I received word that I'd been accepted into the police academy, I could not have been more ecstatic. On the morning of August 2, 1983, I was among the first to arrive for the seventeen-week training. The academy felt a lot like college: attending lectures, taking notes, studying, and plenty of memorizing for test taking, which was my strong suit. The fifty or so of my classmates and I were there to learn the intricacies of the law and the department's procedures. We were also there, through intense daily drills, to get in excellent physical condition and learn how to properly handle a firearm. Before the academy, I'd never even held a gun. When my turn came around to aim and shoot the .38 Smith & Wesson revolver, the sheer force and raw power of each bullet tearing through the air nearly knocked me from my stance.

On day one, I met Walter Williams, a black guy who was then forty-two. At twenty-two, I thought he was old; that notion now makes me laugh. I was the young and dumb one, the baby, while he'd actually experienced a full life. He'd already served for years in the military and was married with children. He'd recently relocated to Dallas from Oklahoma. Despite our age difference, we hit it off right away. We'd joke around between lectures, and on days when the workouts became grueling, we'd challenge each other to stay focused. Like me, Walter had a strong competitive streak. "Man, I bet you can't do a hundred push-ups in less than a minute," he'd say. Seconds later I'd be on the ground, pumping out push-ups while he eyed the clock. During our daily mile runs, he'd always try to outsprint me, and on the few occasions when he did, he wouldn't let me forget it. Much has been said about the strong bond that exists between cops. For Walter and me, that started before we'd officially been declared officers. From our very first conversation, I knew we'd be close friends for life.

We completed our training near the start of the holiday season. Upon graduation, each of us was given a badge and a gun, to be worn alongside an extraordinary sense of duty to serve and protect the residents of the neighborhoods in which we were to be placed. To my surprise, I was assigned to Oak Cliff, and so was Walter. Officers aren't usually assigned to their home neighborhoods, as a way to guard against any favoritism that might arise. I'd listed Oak Cliff as my home on the department application, but that detail was somehow overlooked in an era before records were computerized. Some might have seen that as an administrative oversight. I saw it as divine providence.

I returned to my hometown with no idea of where the assignment would lead me. I only knew that I felt compelled by a profound sense of purpose, one too powerful for me to resist. I hadn't yearned for a life in law enforcement. I'd come back to Oak Cliff simply because everything that I'd ever known and cared about—my family, my home, my community—was at stake. At the time, I thought I was answering the most important call of my life. I'd one day recognize it as only the first.

CHAPTER 2

OAK CLIFF

D ECADES BEFORE I WAS BLESSED WITH THE ASSIGNMENT to serve my neighborhood as a young officer, the story of my family began at Old Parkland. There, at the intersection of Maple and Oak Lawn avenues, Dallas's oldest medical facility was long ago transformed from clapboard house to brick edifice. That original structure later became part of the corporate office complex located there today. Beneath the building's floorboards, layers below the red clay earth, my mom and dad's paths first crossed.

My mother, Norma Jean, and my father, Walter Lee Brown, were born seven months apart—he in 1939, she in 1940. Back then our nation's medical facilities, like its schools and restaurants, were segregated. White parents heard their children's first cries on Old Parkland's upper floors; African-Americans gave birth to their babies in separate quarters. My mother and father, as well as their parents and grandparents, did not begin their lives on floor one or two or four. They were born in the basement.

In October 1960, I also took my first breath at Parkland, but at its new location on Harry Hines Boulevard—the same hospital where, three years after my birth, President Kennedy would be pronounced dead. The country was then in the midst of a social and political ground shift. The Vietnam War drew protests that would crescendo toward a fever pitch of dissent. Though the Supreme Court had mandated the desegregation of schools with the *Brown v. Board of Education* ruling, multiple states, including Texas, fought its implementation. Nine months before my life began, a group of black college students in Greensboro, North Carolina, staged a peaceful demonstration at a Woolworth's lunch counter, demanding the right to be served and thereby launching a movement. Just as it had been during my parents' time and much as it is now, America was at a crossroads.

On a fall day in 2016, I visited the grounds of Old Parkland. A businessman whose workplace is located in the Jeffersonian-style office complex hosted me there for lunch. Our conversation and connection eventually grew into a friendship, and he invited me to set up my postretirement office near him on the fourth floor. On the afternoons when I'm there, I gaze down from my window, past the immaculately groomed courtyard and the mighty oak branches, and whisper a prayer of gratitude for what my family endured to get me here. My parents, their parents, and all the countless ancestors whose names I'll never know paved the way for me. Three generations later and four floors up, I stand proudly on their shoulders.

—

I WAS RAISED BY strong women. Mabel Henderson, my maternal great-grandmother, was my family's matriarch. Her mother and father first settled in Dallas in the early 1900s, along with throngs of other blacks, many of whom migrated to the city in search of work in the city's train yards. I didn't know my great-grandfather; by the time I was born, he had already passed on. But Mabel, with her open heart and warm embrace, lived to age 79. She was a nurturing presence in my life, teaching me to make tea cakes from scratch and to put my trust in the Lord. For more than three decades, she worked as a maid. Every morning she'd board the bus in Oak Cliff and travel to a wealthy area in North Dallas. There she cooked and cleaned for a white family, the Huchensons. At dusk, after a long journey home, she fed her own children and tucked them into bed.

In Mabel's time, the largest African-American enclave was located in lower East Dallas, near the state fair. Other than for work, few blacks ventured out to more affluent neighborhoods. My mother and father both grew up in East Dallas and met as classmates in junior high. My mother, then just twelve, possessed all the quick-witted sass and fashion sense that define her to this day. Mom could piece together the most fashionable ensembles from any assortment of secondhand gems. She was as pretty then as she is now, with pecan-brown skin and delicate features. Smart and well-spoken as she is, one might've never guessed she'd grown up poor. What her family lacked in money, they made up for in dignity, integrity, a strong faith, and an impeccable work ethic—the true measures of class.

At thirteen, my father was already close to six feet tall. His stature, as my mom would tell you, was matched only by his confidence and charisma. Even in early adolescence, he was sharp. He possessed a Miles Davis–inspired swagger: With perfectly trimmed hair and impeccably creased pants, he strode across campus, head up and shoulders square, drawing stares and whispers from the girls. I've never known the story of my parents' first interaction or how they fell for each other. I only know that their connection was instant and unwavering. They dated through high school, and in 1958, with their future laid out before them, they traded vows.

A year into their marriage, Mom and Dad welcomed their first son, my brother Rickey Charles, named after one of my father's favorite singers, Ray Charles. Sixteen months later when I arrived, my mother, a devout Christian, called me David, after the biblical character she admired. My youngest brother, Kelvin, which is just a name my parents loved, was born in the summer of 1963. In the space of five years, my parents had three young mouths to feed on their meager earnings. My father worked in landscaping, and on the side, he pieced together whatever odd jobs he could round up. My mother, who was great with numbers and very organized, worked as a secretary and later as a manager at Mercantile Bank. Finances were tight, to be sure, but they stretched their dollars and extended their workdays in order to make ends meet.

I've always known that both of my parents loved me, but the truth is that my mother did most of the rearing. My father had come from a solid two-parent home. Dad's parents, Roy and Beulah Brown, worked in Dallas's Department of Recreation. They earned a modest income that they spent carefully: My grandfather, a groundskeeper, somehow managed to purchase not only his own home but also the one next door. He and my grandmother may have been of limited means, but their expectations for my dad and his brother, Johnny, were high. They encouraged their sons to apply themselves and strive for better, and though my father tried to live up to that expectation, he could not. He was a good man, yet he didn't help my mother in the ways that I'm sure he wanted and needed to. In the end, trying to be a good man wasn't enough. It left all the burden on my mother.

My father, like scores of black men of his generation, had been relegated to second-class citizenship. He'd come of age in the Jim Crow era, a time when "separate but equal" was code for "alienated and inferior." Landlords legally shunned African-American tenants who applied for housing. Grown men were referred to as boys. Blacks, even those with advanced degrees, were often paid less than their white counterparts. The Civil Rights Act of 1964 officially ended segregation, yet a de facto segregation lingered for many years thereafter. Initially my father conformed to the role in which society had cast him, but over time, he increasingly resented the designation. You weren't going to order my daddy to take a backseat on a bus; if you did, he would dissent by walking instead. You weren't going to tell him he couldn't enroll in a college reserved for whites; if an all-black school was the sole option, he'd refuse to attend rather than indulge the insult.

Though he did not intend it, my father's rebellion ultimately proved detrimental to both him and my mother. In place of doing menial work (which must've felt like an affront to his masculinity), he spent long periods away from home, hanging out, in defiance of a social order that had rendered him insignificant. He continued to earn money by cobbling together work—I never saw my old man broke—and he contributed financially when he could. Even so, my mother, by default, became the primary breadwinner and caregiver. My father was intermittently absent, often for long periods and without explanation to us boys. In hindsight, I respect my father for wanting to be treated like a full man in a world that didn't acknowledge him as such. Yet I wish he would have been around more, particularly for my mom. She longed most not for his wallet but for his daily companionship and emotional support.

And yet my mother never once complained about her heavy load. She sacrificed everything, including a social life, to keep clothes on our backs. She rose before dawn to prepare us for school, and after working all day, she always had a hot meal on the table every evening. At times, she seemed exhausted and alone; some nights, long after she'd put us to bed, I'd hear her softly weeping and praying in the shadows of her bedroom. But at sunup, she'd emerge refortified, wearing a smile and a well-coiffed wig, ready to again take up the task of providing for all of us.

Mabel didn't live with us, but she was close by to support my mother and hold her steady. In every aspect of my upbringing, my great-grandmother's influence could be felt. Nightly around our dinner table, as we bowed our heads and folded our hands in prayer, she was there in spirit if not in flesh, encouraging us to thank the Lord for His merciful provision. When she was there with us, which was frequently, a single sideways glance from either her or my mom could leave me feeling either cherished or chastened, the latter sometimes accompanied by a switch. In the pages of the Old Testament and therefore in our home, to spare the rod was to spoil the child. My brothers and I were neither spoiled nor spared.

Overseeing three knuckleheaded boys could not have been easy. My mother instilled discipline in us by putting the fear of God into us; our healthy fear of her was a close second. Mom's standards for us were exactly the ones she'd been raised with: Respect your elders. Work hard in school, or "get your lessons" as we Southerners say. Keep your surroundings orderly, starting with folding your sheet corners each morning. Always leave home looking neat and tidy. "Don't go out of here with wrinkled clothes," she'd say. And above all other expectations, the one that permeated my upbringing: Aim to do something productive with your life. That notion wasn't necessarily attached to an income or profession. Rather, it was about following the example that my mother, who toiled diligently, set for us. "You don't worry about what anybody else is doing," she'd remind us. "You just stay focused on your goals and do what's right."

I absorbed that wisdom early and applied myself in school accordingly. Even as an elementary school student, I understood that what I did that day could have consequences down the line. My mom says I was born an old soul, a boy peering into the distance and envisioning the road ahead. I was also a child who gravitated toward those who were decades older than me, starting with Mabel. Perhaps from her, I inherited an acute feel for the world around me, an intuition about situations and people. "That child there is up to no good," Mabel would say, assessing a neighbor's son even from a distance. I shared her sense of instinctual recognition. And more than once back then and in the decades since, that awareness would lead to my preservation.

I KNEW WE WERE POOR, yet I didn't grow up feeling that way. I was aware, of course, that Mom didn't have money for extras. In place of Chuck Taylor tennis shoes, the Air Jordans of my day, my brothers and I wore generic-brand sneakers. We didn't have a lot, but we had enough. I'm sure our family qualified for government assistance, but Mom stubbornly refused to go that route. "I'm able-bodied," she'd say. "As long as God gives me the strength, I will work." I did get free lunch at school—as proud as Mom was, she wouldn't let us go hungry—but that was the extent of the help we received.

During all my childhood, we never owned a home or a car; we walked or took the city bus. When I was five, Mom left her job at Mercantile for another at Texas Instruments; she was among the first group of blacks to be hired at the technology company. It was shift work with long hours that involved packing and unpacking parts, but it paid better than her previous job, and she invested her extra income in our education. She sent Rickey and me to a small Catholic school in Oak Cliff. After she had Kelvin, however, her parental responsibilities became too much, and she left the company. Not long after, she began managing apartment buildings. We lived in the buildings she managed, which meant we moved frequently around Oak Cliff. Mom did her job so well that, after a year or two, she'd inevitably be called in to supervise a new facility. Our apartments were usually small two-bedrooms, one room for my mother, the other for my brothers and me. During these years, my dad was not around. For a time when we were quite young, Kelvin and I shared a bunk bed, with me on the bottom since I was a sleepwalker. Rickey was in a bed by himself. As we grew older, we each had our own twin bed. We argued constantly, of course, as siblings do. But while we might've bickered among ourselves, no one who wasn't a Brown could get away with fighting us. Our familial bond was sacrosanct.

My uncle Johnny, my dad's brother, was the most financially successful person in my extended family. For me, he was a role model. He wasn't wealthy, but relative to us, he was well-off. With the help of scholarships and financial aid, he'd attended Prairie View A&M, a historically black university near Houston. He then spent his career as a postman, while his wife, my aunt Gwen, worked as a teacher. They owned a house and a car in a middle-class part of Oak Cliff. There, wood-frame structures known as shotgun homes stood proudly, side by side, in front of manicured lawns. Whenever we'd ride through my aunt and uncle's part of town, I'd stare into the windows of those houses and imagine what it would feel like to one day live in one.

Since we didn't have a home with a backyard, Oak Cliff served as our playground—our athletic field. For all of middle school, my life revolved around sports, from football to track to street basketball. Football might've been the most popular sport in Texas, but in Oak Cliff, it was all about shooting hoops. I didn't look like athlete material. I was the kid with the Payless sneakers, initially dismissed by the other kids. But once I got on that court, I had some ups. These days I can't even jump a foot in the air, but back then I could dunk on you or pin the basketball on the backboard. On the street courts around our neighborhood, I became known for picking players who, like me, looked like they had no game. But if you were on my team, we were going to play our hearts out until the streetlights came on and our parents called us home.

The 1960s Oak Cliff was at once gritty and soulful. As boys played basketball in empty lots and mothers yelled down instructions from their open apartment windows, girls hopscotched and jump-roped atop cracked sidewalks. Old men in suspenders played dominoes and craps on street corners. The voices of Al Green, James Brown, and the Supremes wafted from radio sets. Oak Cliff even had a particular smell, one I still carry with me. The aroma of soul food, of collard greens and fresh biscuits and smothered pork chops, rose to mix with the cackles of friends throwing back their heads in laughter. What probably sounded like loud talk to those passing through was, for those of us who lived there, authentic expression and fellowship. In the air, an aura of warmth and kindness could be felt; neighbors looked out for one another. We were connected not only by the community we inhabited but by the experiences we shared.

I yearn for the Oak Cliff of that era: the people, the smells, the rich heritage. I don't know if the neighborhood appeared to others as it did to me; as author Anaïs Nin once noted, "We don't see things as they are, we see them as we are." In my view, wide-eyed and hopeful, Oak Cliff was a setting in which any dream could take flight, a backdrop to be savored and celebrated.

CHAPTER 3

ROOKIE

———

"WE'VE GOT A CODE FORTY-ONE-ELEVEN, A BURGLARY in progress," I heard on my radio at around ten p.m. "The resident arrived home to find the suspect in her house." An address was given, which happened to be two blocks from the part of Oak Cliff I'd been patrolling. I arrived at the scene seconds later.

As I pulled up, a young man bolted from the front door, carrying a television and an armful of clothes. The moment he spotted a squad car, he dropped everything onto the porch. I stepped out of the car and slowly moved toward him. "Stop and get on the ground!" I shouted. When he and I locked eyes, I immediately recognized him as a former classmate of mine, a kid I'd once shot hoops with years earlier in Oak Cliff. We'd even been on the track team together.

He laughed when he realized he knew me. "Hey, Brown!" he yelled with a smirk on his face. "Let me see if you've still got it!" Then he dropped into a three-point racing stance and took off running across the yard and down the street. I sprinted after him. "Stop and put your hands up!" I ordered. But he kept running, crisscrossing through alleyways and backyards. I stayed right on his tail. As I leaped over fences, my heart pounding away in my chest, all I could think was, *Is this really happening?* Finally, after we'd run about a mile, I got close enough to wrestle him to the ground.

"Man, are you crazy?" I said, gasping for air as I put on the handcuffs. "Why in the world are you running?"

"I just wanted to see if you could still outrun me," he said, snickering at what was no laughing matter, at least not at that moment. I had called for backup, and a squad car soon arrived. Even after we put him in the backseat, he continued hollering. "Boy, you always could run some track!" he screamed.

That's how my year as a rookie began—enforcing the law in a place where I knew, or at least knew of, just about everybody. When some of my friends and neighbors heard I'd joined the force, they labeled me an Uncle Tom. That didn't bother me at all, mostly because I understood the divine nature of the call I'd answered. I understood that call was between me and the Lord.

Others expressed their pride and often told me, "Stay safe— the world out there is dangerous." It can get dicey serving the neighborhood you've grown up in. I often had to write tickets for people I liked or, worse, imprison those who'd gotten caught up in criminal activity. But I felt no conflict. I'd been placed there to protect the lives and property of residents in a community I loved. That commitment energized me, particularly during my initial months on the force, when crack's impact on the city was growing more powerful and damaging by the day.

After I'd graduated from the academy and completed three months of on-the-job training, I was put on the night shift—2:30 p.m to 10:30 p.m. Most rookies are assigned to that shift, the least desirable time frame because it doesn't allow for much of a social life. In our first few weeks on the beat in Oak Cliff's Southwest Patrol Division, my buddy Walter and I often rode together as partners. For the first four hours, one of us took the wheel while the other handled all the calls and paperwork—and then halfway through, we'd switch roles. "You want to drive first tonight?" he'd sometimes ask me at the start of our shift. The answer was always yes. I loved driving and couldn't stand filling out all those forms.

Walter and I rode together for a few months before I went solo. As much as I enjoyed our partnership, I am independent by nature. These days many young cops want to ride in pairs; they feel more secure that way. But in my generation, we were old-school John Wayne types, full of bravado. Patrolling alone was a rite of passage, a way of proving you could handle your beat, which I knew I could since I was in my old stomping grounds. And yet even after Walter and I separated, we talked all the time. We began every morning with the same conversation.

"Hey, man," I'd say. "What's going on?"

"I made three arrests yesterday," he'd say. "How many did you make?"

"I actually put four people in jail," I'd announce, proud to have outdone him. In our competition, catching a burglar earned you more credibility than, say, writing five speeding tickets. For us, it was all about tracking down the biggest felons and sending them off to prison.

When Walter and I weren't trading notes on the previous shift's happenings, we were planning how we could move up the ranks in our department. "You could easily pass the test to become a sergeant," I once told him after we'd been on the force for about a year. "And I could see either of us becoming chief one day," he responded. "Nah, man, that's not for me," I said, laughing. "I'm all for getting promoted, but I'll leave the politics to some other fool." That was in 1984. Even then I knew what I was and wasn't good at. "We can just work our way up to captain," I told him. But he persisted. "One of us needs to be chief," he said. For Walter, that was an aspiration worth aiming for—the very top job.

CHAPTER 4

CHOICES

——

A GROUP OF TEACHERS AND ADMINISTRATORS CONGRE-
gated in a corner of the school cafeteria. The year was
1967. I was seven and there for my first day in second grade.
Segregation still the unofficial order of the day, throughout elementary school, I attended all-black schools. On that morning
at Roger Q. Mills in east Oak Cliff, my classmates paid little
attention to the adults huddling. I, ever the observer, tuned in
to the conversation.

"So which children should we choose?" one of them said.
These teachers in the cafeteria were deciding how to organize
us. With their backs turned, they had no idea I could hear them.

"Who are the smartest kids on this list?" the principal asked.
They glanced down at a sheet that bore the students' names.
"This one is a strong reader," someone said, pointing toward
the top of the paper. Other names were mentioned, but I wasn't
close enough to catch them all.

Not long after, the teachers gathered us and then separated us into groups of about fifteen. The teacher for my group, a young petite black woman, led us to her classroom. There we crowded into a semicircle around her desk. About ten of the students were girls; I was among the handful of boys.

The teacher stood and walked to the front of the desk, closer to us. She leaned toward us. "Now listen to me," she said. "You-all are the smartest kids in the school." A couple of my class-mates giggled and exchanged a glance before looking back at her. "I want you to know that I'm going to challenge you every day," she continued. "I expect you to work hard. I expect you to sit at the front of the class every chance you get. And I expect you to be the first to answer questions."

I don't recall that teacher's name, but with a single sentence, she changed the way I saw myself. I'd enjoyed school up to then, but that morning at Roger Q. Mills was the first time a teacher had explicitly told me "You are smart." Those three words not only took root in my heart; they sparked in me an even stronger passion for learning, a conviction to always do my best.

In that environment of heightened expectations, school came easily for me. My mom recalls that I had a nearly photographic memory. I also listened far more than I talked; I'd memorize everything my teachers said in class and then later reproduce it during exams. That ability to capture and recall much of what I heard made me well suited for the performing arts. In those years, our school district emphasized the arts. Every child had to be in choir and theater. Some of my classmates would struggle to recall their lyrics and lines, but I was a human wiretap; I could hear a song or script once and deliver it almost perfectly a short time later. And let me tell you, quiet as I was, I loved to perform.

I'm going to lose all my street cred when I admit this, but in third grade, I auditioned for and landed the role of Captain von Trapp in *The Sound of Music*. After a couple weeks of rehearsal, I took the stage, clad in a military jacket with shiny gold buttons, and sang my first solo, "Edelweiss." Later, during the show's finale, I belted out a full-throated rendition of "Climb Ev'ry Mountain." I sang my heart out, as if convinced I was actually escaping with Maria and our children through the Alps. My teachers must have been equally convinced, because from then on, I landed nearly every lead in our school's plays. Theater taught me how to convey a message, short and sweet, through words and music. It also did what academics alone seldom do: It brought me out of my shell. By the end of that school year, I went from reticent and aloof to comfortable in my skin. I felt as confident on the stage as I did in the classroom.

AFTER MY BROTHERS AND I completed our homework on weekday evenings, Mom allowed us to turn on our old RCA television. From my spot on the living-room couch, I'd watch all the cop and superhero shows. *Dragnet,* starring L.A. police sergeant Joe Friday. *Batman* and *Superman. Columbo,* the homicide detective. *The Mod Squad,* a trio of undercover police. I enjoyed the action, the law and order, the danger and drama, the way the hero came swooping in, cape on his back, to save lives and restore justice.

On weekends at Mabel's house, I loved watching *Perry Mason,* the courtroom drama; my great-grandmother watched the series with such regular devotion that, even now, I can recall many of the episodes. Perry, a defense attorney of pristine character, took on seemingly hopeless cases and then deftly proved his clients' innocence. I knew Perry wasn't an actual person, but to me, he felt like one. I found everything about him appealing: his professionalism, his debonair suits and cool demeanor, his steadfast pursuit of the truth, and especially the way he served others in their greatest hour of need. Long after Mabel turned off the television and I lay in bed, drifting off to sleep, I dreamed not of becoming a cop or a detective but of one day serving as a defense attorney—a black Perry Mason.

And yet as much as those fictional characters shaped my earliest aspirations, none held as much sway as the two powerful women who raised me. In my mother's lap and on Mabel's knee, under their watchful gaze and in their tender words and embrace, I discovered true strength and resilience and a desire to excel. They, the towering figures of my childhood, were the real heroes.

I WAS DETERMINED TO PLAY running back on my fifth-grade football team. I was somewhat scrawny then and not very tall. Even today I'm an average five foot ten. But man, was I competitive. When I'd catch a pass, I'd take off running with that ball as if I'd just stolen it. The fact that there were a hundred other boys trying out for the team didn't deter me; it actually strengthened my resolve.

"Line up!" shouted Coach Hulcy on the field at Elisha M. Pease Elementary. That year, after Mom landed a job in a new apartment building in another area of Oak Cliff, I'd switched elementary schools. Like the previous ones, this one was all black. Coach Hulcy, a slender man with brown hair and kind eyes, was white.

Those of us who'd been waiting on the sidelines formed a line, and he directed us to one end of the field to begin some drills. He, carrying three or four footballs, took a spot at the other end. He wanted to see which of us could catch and throw and how fast we were. "Let's see what you've got!" he said, throwing the first ball toward the kid near the front of the group. The boy caught the ball and threw it back perfectly. When my turn came, I caught the ball and dropped it. On my second go-round, I knew I had to regroup and demonstrate my skills. So I ran a straight fly pattern down the field, caught the pass, and then . . . I fumbled it again. When this happened three more times, I was so frustrated with myself that I palmed that ball and hurled it back to the coach. At least, though angry, I'd actually completed the pass.

One by one Coach Hulcy began cutting boys. He yelled out a name. Then another. Then five more. "Good try," he'd say, "but I'm sorry, I can't use you this year." Meanwhile I continued dropping most of my passes, and the few I did return, I threw hard. I had never been more emotional; every time the ball fell from my grip, tears threatened to spill from my eyes. I had never wanted anything more than I wanted to make that team. It meant everything to me.

A short time later I heard the words I'd been dreading. "Brown, get over here!" shouted the coach. As I dragged myself toward him, my head lowered, I tried with all my might not to break down; the only thing worse than getting cut from the team was being labeled a crybaby by my classmates. I kept my eyes glued to the grass beneath my feet.

When the coach didn't speak for what felt like an eternity, I finally looked up at him. He was handing me a football.

"You're my quarterback," he told me.

I stared at him. "What?" I mumbled.

"I want you on the team," he said. "You're in."

"Really?" I said in disbelief.

"Yes, really," he said. "Now get back out there before I change my mind."

Not only was I chosen as quarterback that year, I also served as captain of the team. Coach Hulcy later told me why he'd picked me. He'd of course seen me dropping every pass, but he'd also noticed something else: When I'd returned the ball to him at my moment of greatest frustration, I'd thrown it so hard that it landed in his hands in a tight spiral. I'd been focused on my weakness; he'd been focused on my strong suit.

We did not lose a single game that fall; my teammates and I still call it our Cinderella season. Our victories had as much to do with the kind of man Coach Hulcy was as with the athletic skills he helped us to refine. He cared about us and coached us as if we were his sons, pushing us to challenge ourselves as well as to value fair play and sportsmanship. Even after that school year was finished, he kept in touch with us, extolling our successes both on and off the field, sharing with us the gift of his encouragement. He left me with a lesson that would be proven time and again in the decades ahead: Your biggest failures and greatest successes can happen on the same field.

I WAS BUSED AS a sixth grader. Dallas's first attempt at integration, the so-called stair-step plan, was put in place to gradually desegregate the district. It was 1971. The plan did not go over well, particularly among white residents, and the result was a palpable sense of anxiety and racial tension. I was among the first group of kids to be sent to Mark Twain, then a predominantly white elementary school in south Oak Cliff. Rickey was bused to a middle school.

The experience was painful from day one. "Hi," I'd say to a classmate, only to have him or her completely ignore me. No one had to spit on me; they did so with their stares and smirks or, worse, by averting their eyes as if my presence weren't even worth noting. Words were not necessary. Their demeanors communicated their silent contempt and disdain: *We don't want you here.* In their eyes, I was at once profoundly offensive and wholly invisible. Most of the time, I sat alone in the lunchroom or with the handful of other black children forced to attend this school. What was intended as integration felt more to me like quarantine.

One afternoon about three months into that school year, I stood awaiting my bus ride home. A blond kid shuffled toward me. I recognized him as Mike Shillingburg, one of the most popular guys in the school—in other words, the last person who'd ever talk to someone like me. The hairs on the back of my neck stood up as he drew closer. I didn't want any trouble.

"Hey, man," he said. "You want to come to my house for dinner?"

I stared at him for a long moment and didn't answer. *Is he talking to me?* I thought. *Did I hear him right?* Using the strong instincts I'd inherited from my great-grandmother, I looked directly into his blue eyes, searching for ill intent or mockery. I sensed neither. "Okay," I muttered without giving it much more thought. "I'll come." I picked up my backpack and began walking alongside him.

Mike lived only a few blocks from the school. When we arrived at his home, his mother met us at the front door.

"Hello, my dear," she welcomed Mike. A half second later, her eyes darted from him to me, as if to say, *Who have we here?* Mike apparently hadn't told his mom he was bringing company, and even if he had, she clearly wasn't expecting a black person. Mike introduced me as his classmate. I felt like Sidney Poitier in *Guess Who's Coming to Dinner?* She said, "Um, hi, David—come on in."

I took a place on their living-room couch after Mike and his mother excused themselves to the kitchen. I overheard them whispering and wondered how long it would take for me to be kicked out. They soon reappeared, and Mike's mom was carrying a tray of delicious-smelling food. "Let's have dinner," she said, offering me a seat at the table. As I made my way to my chair, I thought, *White people sure do eat dinner early*. It was three p.m. In my house, we never ate before seven.

The initial awkwardness of the visit quickly disappeared as Mike and I dove into our dinner. Between bites, we talked nonstop about everything from football to the cutest girls at school. If someone had witnessed our conversation, they would've assumed we'd known each other for years rather than a half hour. The conversation just flowed. In fact, it flowed so well that I lost track of time. Two hours passed before I remembered I hadn't told anyone where I was. This was in the days before cellphones, and probably because I, like many kids my age, didn't think to do the obvious, I neglected to use Mike's home phone to ring my mother. I also had no ride back to my neighborhood. That bus I'd skipped was long gone.

"I can take you home," Mike's mother offered. "We'll all

ride over together." I thought to myself, *You're gonna drive me to the 'hood?* But given that I had no other option, I went along with it. A half hour later, just as the sun was setting, she and Mike dropped me off at the front of our apartment building. When they sped off, a cloud of dust formed—I'd never seen a white woman drive so fast in my life.

I walked to the back of the complex, where our apartment was located. As I got closer, I noticed a couple hundred people gathered in the center courtyard. With her back toward me, my mother was addressing the crowd. When she noticed me from the corner of her eye, she turned around and leaped toward me, throwing her arms all the way around me. "My baby!" she wailed. "What happened to you?"

When I didn't arrive home on my usual bus, Mom had panicked. At a time when opponents of forced busing were expressing outrage, she was sure the Klan had somehow gotten to me. As the minutes of my absence ticked by, she'd become more and more sure she'd never see me again. In desperation, she'd hurriedly organized a search party among our family and neighbors.

After Mom composed herself, she launched into an inquisition. "Where have you been?" she asked.

"I—uh—" I stammered, "I had dinner at Mike Shillingburg's house."

She gaped at me. In the next moment, my mother, who'd never uttered a curse word in front of me, shouted at the top of her voice, "And who the hell is Mike Shillingburg?"

"Well, I mean . . . he's my friend," I explained.

"Your *friend*?" she said. "You don't know anybody at that school!" A few people in the crowd snickered, which thankfully cut the tension. Mom then hugged me a second time, this time even tighter. "Don't you ever do that to me again, you hear me?" she said. "I'm just glad you're all right."

From that day onward, Mike and I were inseparable. He was so well liked around school that those who'd shunned me began warming up to me, simply because he'd become my friend. We eventually campaigned for student council together, he for class president and I for his vice president. Following our victory, we hosted events and social gatherings in an effort to unite our classmates across racial lines. It was more than a friendship; it was, for me, an opportunity to see the world through a different lens.

Mike moderated my views on race. Before meeting him, I'd seen whites through the only filter I had then, one created by the humiliation I'd endured early in that school year. His invitation to dinner changed that for me. If he hadn't asked me to come home with him that day, my lifelong internal narrative about whites might have been *You treated me like dirt, all of you did. I want nothing to do with you.* But after he befriended me, my perspective became, *You invited me home to dinner. Some of you treated me poorly, but one of you embraced me.* As our friendship grew, we used our connection to bring our classmates together. And along the way, I discovered what I still know—that we're all far more alike than we are different.

Mike and I eventually went on to different schools and fell out of touch. But decades after we'd first connected, we reunited. As we reminisced about our sixth-grade year, I realized he'd had no idea back then that our friendship had meant so much to me. That day at the bus stop, he'd approached me not because he was aware of what I was going through but because he thought I seemed like a cool kid. His invitation wasn't born of pity. It was an extension of kindness—a sincere act of warmth that altered my path.

I GREW UP IN church. For most of my early childhood, we traveled to South Dallas to attend one that was traditional Baptist. It was the kind of congregation where deacons knelt along the front pew to lead the morning devotion, where grandmothers in colorful hats shouted "Amen!," where the choir's voices blended with the sounds of the tambourine and wafted toward heaven as the preacher caught the Spirit. There were about a hundred members, half of whom attended every Sunday. We were among those who came when we could make it, which was not every week. My mother's best friend, Emma, and Emma's husband, Sonny, had been the ones who invited us, and they always offered us a ride, since they knew we didn't have a car. But Mom didn't want to impose.

I was around thirteen when Mom began looking for a church close to us in east Oak Cliff. We visited a few local places of worship, but for most of that year, we were between congregations. That didn't mean the biblical teachings halted, though. After dinner some evenings, Mom would pull out her New Testament and read Scripture to us. She also prayed constantly. Often before daybreak, I could hear her thanking the good Lord for yet another day.

Christ for the Nations, an international Christian nonprofit organization, moved into our neighborhood that year. It bought a building adjacent to ours and housed dozens of missionaries there. You couldn't walk down the block without one of them approaching. One spring afternoon when I was on my way to a pickup basketball game, a young brunette woman came up to me.

"Have you accepted Jesus as your Lord and Savior?" she asked.

I stared at her. *You must not know my mama,* I thought. "Well," I said, "I've been going to church since I was young."

She smiled and nodded. "But do you know Jesus?" she said.

"Uh, yes," I said, shrugging. "I guess so."

Right there on that street corner, we got into a long conversation about faith and repentance, grace and forgiveness. She asked me about several passages in the Bible that, surprisingly, I'd never heard. While sitting in church all those years, fidgeting in the pews, I hadn't been tuning in to much of what the preacher was saying. I had been there because, in Norma Jean's house, there was no choice but to attend. That missionary got me thinking about what I truly believed. Were my beliefs real for me?

I thanked the woman and headed toward my game. As I played, I couldn't get our conversation off my mind. *Do I really take this religion thing seriously?* I didn't say anything about it to my buddies; I just mulled it over quietly. Even as I left the court a couple hours later and walked home alone, I was still thinking about it.

I arrived at our complex. Instead of immediately going upstairs, I made my way slowly around the perimeter of our building. I began whispering the prayer of salvation, the one the missionary had given me. "Lord," I prayed, "please forgive me for my sins and come into my heart." When I was halfway around the complex, it started to drizzle. Not long after, it began to pour. By the time I'd circled back to our apartment, I was drenched. I'd also made the most important decision of my life. As I often say now, I was saved by grace and baptized in the rain.

As I entered our apartment that evening, I didn't know much more about God or the Bible than I'd known previously. The clouds hadn't parted and the Earth hadn't trembled when I'd prayed my salvation prayer. But on that afternoon in 1973, the faith that had always belonged to my mother became my own. It was personal, between me and the Lord.

I DETEST THE SMELL of cigarette smoke. So when one of my basketball teammates lit up and inhaled a joint, which I thought was a cigarette, my instinct was to bolt.

"Hey, man," he said. "You should try this."

"No, that's okay," I said. But when he insisted, I took the joint, put it right up to my lips, and began to cough. Within seconds, I felt nauseous and light-headed, as if my brain were about to explode.

"What is this stuff?" I said, handing it back to him.

"It's weed," he said. "Haven't you ever tried it?"

I hadn't. In fact, up to then, I'd never even seen it. I'd heard about marijuana and sometimes smelled a scent on street corners and in alleyways that I thought might be pot, but I'd never made the connection. It was the nastiest thing I'd ever tasted.

The year was 1975. During my second semester in eighth grade, my mother, Kelvin, and I had moved to San Francisco. Mabel had relocated first; for years, one of her granddaughters there had been begging her to come and stay, and she'd finally relented. Mom couldn't bear the thought of being so far from her beloved grandmother, so she arranged for us to go along. Rickey, who was in tenth grade at the time, stayed in Dallas. He had been accepted to the Booker T. Washington High School for the Performing and Visual Arts and wanted to finish his program. Mom allowed him to live with Uncle Johnny and Aunt Gwen. Upon arriving in California, Mom found administrative work right away, and we moved into an apartment in the Fillmore District, then a tough part of town. I enrolled at Marina Middle School and, of course, joined the basketball team.

San Francisco could not have been more different from Dallas: the climate, the terrain, the culture, the racial mix. I was one of a handful of blacks in class; the majority of the students were either white or Asian, with a fairly equal split between those two groups. On the playground, everything except the basketball court was covered in sand. It was the strangest thing, as was my classmates' perception of me. Back home, I'd considered myself an inner-city kid, shooting hoops and talking trash with my buddies. But in California, I was seen as a country kid. "Hey, Texas," some of my classmates would jokingly greet me in a Southern drawl. "Where'd you say you was from? Dallas?" I was unfazed. But all the teasing ended on the basketball court. I earned my cred by kicking some tail.

On the afternoon my teammate offered me pot, it is only by the grace of God that I didn't like it. Still, I could have succumbed to peer pressure. I could have pretended to enjoy it just to fit in. But thanks to my mother and Mabel, I had the strength to refuse simply because it did not feel right to me. I'd always been a fussy kid, even about what food I ate; if I didn't like something, I'd push it aside. My mother would have been sorely disappointed if she'd known I'd even put a joint up to my mouth.

I've often wondered how my life would have turned out differently if I'd taken a puff and enjoyed it. My experimentation would probably not have ended with weed. I never do anything halfway; I'm always all in. I would have moved on to more potent drugs. Thank God that, as a young kid with an old soul, I understood that if I wanted to get out of poverty and land a decent job one day, I couldn't be high. I had to be sober and near perfect to have even a small chance. All our lives come with a series of defining moments, those pivot points at which our decision to go left, turn right, or remain still determines all that will come after. For me, this was one such turning point. From where we stand now, with marijuana legalization taking hold throughout the country, things look different. But if I had become a marijuana user back in 1975, the option to become a police officer likely would not have been there for me.

We stayed in San Francisco for about eighteen months and returned to Dallas at the start of my tenth-grade year. Mom missed her life in Texas more than she'd thought she would, and I did too. I was overjoyed to reconnect with my friends and settle into familiar surroundings. Though our time in California had been relatively short, I came home a different kid—one who'd been exposed to a world beyond the only one I'd ever experienced. No longer did I see Oak Cliff as the entirety of my existence.

CHAPTER 5

LOCK 'EM UP

—

I COULD EASILY IDENTIFY A DRUG HOUSE. UPON ARRIVING AT a suspected dealer's home, I'd start looking around on the ground or picking through the trash can in search of paraphernalia. Dozens of needles? Check. Razor blades, glass pipes, syringes, plastic baggies? All telltale signs. Whenever I'd have a lull during my shift in my first few years on the force, I'd drive over to the vicinity of a house I had my eye on, stake out a spot at the end of the block, and just wait for the inevitable to happen— a traffic violation.

While in the academy, I'd memorized the traffic code; most of us can't drive two blocks without breaking it. Running a red light, pushing forty in a thirty-miles-per-hour residential zone, failing to stop before backing out of a driveway—they all count as violations. In the case of that last one, drug users were notorious offenders. They were usually in such a hurry to make their purchase, get home, and shoot up that they sped out of their dealers' driveways. Others, whose addictions rendered them inattentive to details, failed to notice that one of their headlights had gone out. Either scenario created the probable cause I needed to pull over a driver, and when I did, he or she often had drugs or stolen property in the car.

One summer evening I stopped a young guy who'd absolutely floored it while backing out of a driveway. "May I see your license and registration?" I asked him.

"I don't have it with me," he said. That was a red flag; in my experience, people involved in criminal activity often did not carry ID because they didn't want to be identified. I asked him his name. He gave me one that sounded pretty generic. I doubted it was his real name. I then asked for his full birth date.

"It's December eighteenth, nineteen sixty-two," he said without looking at me.

"So how old are you?" I shot back.

He paused. "I'm twenty-three."

Wrong answer—that birth date would have made him twenty-two. Having caught him in a lie, I charged and arrested him for his various traffic violations and then conducted a custody search of his vehicle. I discovered the drugs he'd purchased and took him to the county jail. There his fingerprints revealed why he'd given me a fake name and birth date. There was an outstanding warrant for his arrest.

In those days, I pulled over and arrested drug users by the dozens. When I was on the clock, you couldn't back out of the lot of a crack house without getting stopped by me. And I didn't stay on the lookout just for the lone addict, the little guy determined to get his fix on a Friday night. I also had my eye on the suppliers and dealers—the players behind the scenes. In one case, my appetite put them right in my path.

"May I have a chopped beef sandwich?" I asked the man at the counter of the barbecue shop where I'd stopped for my evening meal.

He stared at me. "We're out of that," he finally said.

I stepped back from the counter and peered up at the large menu above the register. "How about the hot link basket or the barbecue chicken?" I asked.

"We don't have those today," he said.

"What *do* you have?" I asked, puzzled about how a barbecue house could be out of its main menu items.

"We don't have very much in stock right now," he told me. "We're expecting a new shipment tomorrow."

I thanked the cashier and left. On my way out, I walked around to the back of the shop and checked the trash bin. It was filled with drug paraphernalia of every variety. This place wasn't a legit barbecue joint; it was a front for a major drug business. From the looks of the garbage, the owner was selling everything from marijuana to crack.

I returned to my car, drove to the end of the street, and waited for someone to pull out too fast from the restaurant's lot. Minutes later I pulled over a man in his early twenties.

"What's going on in that barbecue house?" I asked him.

"Um, nothing," he stammered. "I mean, uh . . . what do you mean, sir?"

"Come on, brotha, don't try and play me," I said sternly. "Now, don't make me take you to jail. Are they selling drugs in that restaurant?"

He nodded, and without further inquisition, I let the tipster drive off. I then called the narcotics division to report the drug house. "Can you-all help me shut down this place?" I asked the detective. An undercover agent was sent in to make several buys, and those interactions served as sufficient evidence for a judge to issue a warrant. Within weeks, a SWAT team rolled in to bust the dealers. I would later learn that dealers and building owners were often coconspirators in their scheme. Dealers would offer to pay a landlord double the monthly rent if he or she'd agree to keep quiet about what went on there. When such complicity could be proven in a lawsuit, the owner could be charged with a criminal offense, and the city had the right to take possession of the property.

That incident helped me begin connecting the dots: Excellent policing is *strategic* and *thoughtful* policing—an approach that keeps the big picture in focus. Locking up individual addicts could seem a necessary part of the job. Yet for every five drug users I put in jail, another five emerged. A few days later the same five I'd helped lock away were often back on the streets, using again. It felt like chasing my tail. I began to realize that it wasn't enough to simply arrest addicts; we had to cut off the supply chain. (Years later I'd discover that even that approach falls way short. The drug epidemic isn't about supply. It's about demand. Drug houses exist only because customers keep buying. And as long as there's a strong market, suppliers and dealers will remain in business.)

Still, fueled by all the pent-up energy I'd carried since the summer I'd first witnessed Oak Cliff in disaster, I made it my personal mission to shut down as many drug operations as I could. If you've ever lived next to a drug house or in a neighborhood inundated with drugs, you understand how important this work is. And let me tell you, I devastated the crack houses on my beat. One by one they were closed down—sometimes even bulldozed. And slowly, bit by bit, grandmothers and sisters and daughters could walk a little more freely to the street corner, even if just for a few days or weeks. You don't stop a crack epidemic overnight; nor can you address it using a singular tactic. But as a patrol officer who was one part of the equation during the War on Drugs in the 1980s, my approach was straightforward: Put the criminals in jail, and let God sort them out.

COPS LIVE ON ALERT. While you're patrolling the streets and answering calls, and even when you're not, you're in defense mode. You have to maintain an awareness of your surroundings at all times. And if anything happens, you've got to be ready to respond appropriately. Take your focus off a situation for even a second, and someone could end up dead. Officers are there to protect the people of their cities; that is our duty, first and foremost. But from the moment you join the force, you're also strongly guided by one of the primal urges that unites us as humans: survival. The desire to stay alive cuts across all racial, cultural, and socioeconomic lines.

In part, this instinct explains officers' skewed view of the world: We see life through the prism of possibilities, not probabilities. Let's say I'm out patrolling, and I notice your car swerve. I pull you over. As you slow down, I see you reach down and pick something up. The average person considers the likely reasons you bent forward: Chances are, you dropped your cellphone or water bottle and want to retrieve it, or you're just nervous about being stopped by an officer. Of course, those are probabilities. But it's also possible that you swerved because you're a dangerous armed felon with warrants for your arrest, and when you realized you were being pulled over, you bent down to reach for your gun. I have to proceed as if that possibility is in play until I can rule it out. And it's why I would approach your car with my gun drawn. As a cop, dealing in probabilities could cost me my life. Dealing in possibilities could save it.

I've seen this perspective shape officers' actions even when they aren't on the job. Once a month for many years now, one of my mentors, an eighty-year-old retired cop, has met me for lunch. If he gets there first, he always takes a seat facing the door. Why? Because it is *possible* that the place will be robbed. It is possible that, with his back turned, an active shooter could roll in and launch into a murderous rampage. "If somebody does rob the place," I tease him, "what are you going to do? I'm the one with the gun and holster." My friend has been off the force for more than thirty years, yet he hasn't been cured of the instinct to stay hypervigilant. That's how hardwired the habit can be.

The heartbreaking calls you answer as a police officer can heighten this sense of hypervigilance and its corresponding anxiety. There are approximately 2.5 million residents in Dallas proper, and officers respond to an estimated two million emergency calls every year. Those 911 calls represent one slice of the general public—the slice that is facing crisis. People don't call you when they're relaxing on their deck, sipping a margarita. They call you when someone's dying. When they're being robbed. When all hell has broken loose. Early during my time on the force, I was once called to the scene of an auto accident on the freeway. Two cars had collided, and both had over-turned. There, in the backseat of the Chevy, I peered in to see two toddlers still strapped in their car seats, their bodies mangled and lifeless.

After we filed our paperwork on a call like that, we had to answer the next call, and the ten after that. There was no down-time. There were no moments to process the horrors we'd just witnessed, no therapist or priest to talk with between one crime scene and another. Some of us would be pulling up to handle another sad situation, still distraught over what we'd just seen, and we wouldn't dare show it. In our profession, that would be considered a sign of weakness. We didn't complain. We didn't play crybaby or whiner or victim. We just put a tight lid over our emotions and moved forward. That was the job we'd signed up for. Somebody had to be there to answer the next urgent call. Even in later decades, when more resources became available in some of the nation's large police departments, the stiff-upper-lip culture persisted.

I FOUND A WAY TO COPE. My involvement in church served as a lifeline. Back when I was attending college in Austin, I tuned in to a radio broadcast called *The Urban Alternative,* produced by Dr. Tony Evans, pastor of Oak Cliff Bible Fellowship. I enjoyed the broadcast so much that when I returned to Dallas, I immediately joined that church. As a rookie, I quickly discovered that I couldn't fight my own battles or carry my own burdens; in order to sustain myself, I had to lay my burdens at the feet of the Lord. That belief and practice mitigated my hypervigilance. My connection to the church, my friends, and my community was what kept me sane. I also didn't think or re-spond like a cop 24/7. When I wasn't working, I didn't carry a gun. Unlike many of my colleagues on the force who socialized only with other cops, I intentionally nurtured friendships with those who were not on the force and who lived in the commu-nity I patrolled and served. To continue my work for years on end, I knew I needed a separation between my personal and professional worlds. I aimed for balance—which is an enor-mous challenge when you're on the clock as much as I was.

I worked constantly during those years. I usually put in about eighty hours a week, the equivalent of two full-time po-sitions. In addition to my job as a beat cop, I held down various side gigs: security officer at a restaurant, a bank, an apartment complex. The extra income not only provided a comfortable lifestyle for my family, it allowed me to begin saving toward a home. In between moonlighting and patrolling, I also resumed my college course work. I enrolled at UT Arlington, which was near my patrol station. After one semester, however, I had to quit because I was just too busy with work.

In retrospect, I'd call myself a workaholic, though I didn't feel like one at the time. I had given myself over to a passionate pursuit, one I found exciting and fulfilling, even with its diffi-culties and dangers. From the beginning, I was enamored with policing. On a daily basis, I could change people's lives in a real and meaningful way. If a guy was beating his wife, I could ar-rest him and send him away to jail, all while threatening him that he'd see my face again if he ever laid another finger on the woman. If a teenager was on the verge of suicide, I could show up and sometimes talk the teen and the parents into reaching out for professional support. I was upholding the vow I'd made to serve—and in many cases, that involved saving lives.

Late one night during the graveyard shift, I answered a domestic violence call from a woman who was being beaten by her boyfriend. On the call, the kids could be heard crying in the background. When my partner and I, Hiram Burleson, arrived, the boyfriend met us at the door. He stood blocking the entryway with his hand posted high against the doorjamb. He was shirtless and sweating profusely.

"Everything okay?" I asked. "We're fine," he told us. But behind him in the living room, I could see the woman and her kids sitting quietly, trembling as if they were afraid for their lives. As my partner was about to push the boyfriend aside and walk in to talk with the woman, I noticed a knife in the boyfriend's raised hand. "Drop the knife!" I said, drawing my weapon. He didn't comply. Instead, he lunged at us with the blade. While some cops might've just shot him, we fought him down to the ground as she screamed for him to stop. "Please don't kill him!" the woman shrieked. We finally got control of him and took away the knife. Then we arrested him and took him to jail.

MOST OF THE COPS I know joined the profession for the same reason that I did: to save the world, or at least our corner of it. That's what both Walter and I wanted more than anything. We knew we'd never make much money. We also knew we'd be criticized. And yet even now, at a time when tensions between officers and the communities they serve have never been higher, people are still putting in applications for this job. That is because the desire to serve, to rise up as a hero for others, can be powerful enough to eclipse all concerns. It was strong enough to transform me, the great-grandson of a maid, into a foot soldier for the community that produced me.

IN EARLY 1988, the Dallas Police Department, the DPD, created a new police rank—senior corporal. As soon as Walter and I heard about the position, which came with a 5 percent raise, we began preparing to take the exam so that we'd be among the first to get promoted. We studied together every day before work. Weeks later our efforts paid off when we both passed with flying colors. Once you become a senior corporal, you're assigned to other divisions within the department. I put in a request to become a crime scene detective.

Walter had different plans. "I want to be a field trainer," he told me.

"Why in the world would you want to do that?" I asked him, puzzled about why he'd choose such a difficult and risky job. Field trainers are the officers who train and ride with new cops. "Those rookies make too many mistakes," I told him. "There's no telling what they'll do in a crisis."

But Walter had his mind made up. "Somebody's gotta be there to bring up the next generation of cops," he said. We left it at that.

Both of us were assigned to our desired posts, and I could see how much he enjoyed his job. Our morning conversations returned to the topics we'd always talked about—how we could one day climb to the DPD's highest ranks. "If I'm ever at the helm of this department," he'd tell me, "let me tell you how I'd run things." He'd then expound on the details of his vision, listing the things he'd do differently. He'd hold officers accountable for unethical behavior. He'd be tough on violent felons.

My learning curve as a crime scene investigator was long and steep. Before I investigated my first case, an expert was brought in to teach me and my colleagues all there is to know about gathering forensic evidence: how to properly dust for fingerprints at burglary, robbery, and homicide scenes (you need to get enough of the palm or the upper part of a thumb or right index finger to be able to count and examine its unique lines and grooves through a magnifying glass); how to photograph a dead body and determine the probable cause of death; and how to gather and secure any evidence that might eventually help prove a court case. When someone has been shot or stabbed, for instance, the way his or her blood splatters onto the ground reveals part of the story of what happened. That splatter points the detective in the direction the wounded person may have been moving. Wherever the splatter ends is likely where the person escaped—into a car or a structure in the vicinity. As an investigator, you snap photographs as you look around for anyplace where the splatter might pick up. As a beat cop, you do none of these tasks. In that role, your primary job is to answer calls and take reports, which you then hand off to an investigative unit. As a newbie to CSI, I was a sponge. I soaked up every secret I could.

I also saw a lot of dead bodies. My three-year tenure as an investigator happened to coincide with the era in which Dallas's crime rate was at its height: just over four hundred murders a year. Today it's less than half that. Most of the deaths back then were drug-related; many were African-American men. I witnessed the ugliest side of law enforcement. I confronted heart-break and death on almost a daily basis.

Death has a unique smell to it—a stench that hangs in the air long after a body has been carried off to the morgue. The smell gets in your clothes. On your hands. In your pores. Hours after I'd leaned over a corpse to photograph it, I'd be eating dinner and still smelling that pungent odor. The only thing more pow-erful than that smell were the gut-wrenching reactions of those whose loved ones had been killed. Although I wasn't the one to notify family members, they were often present at the scenes I investigated. You never forget a mother's guttural howl, that sound she releases when she has just received news that her baby is gone. Even the most callous cop can be moved to tears. It's a shriek born purely of love and grief, never of judgment, even when that mother's child has been on the wrong side of the law.

Holidays were the hardest—that's when the number of sui-cide calls spikes significantly. Every year starting just before Thanksgiving and extending through Christmas and New Year's Day, I'd dread starting my night shift. It's nauseating to witness slashed wrists, bloated bodies floating in bathtubs, bul-let wounds to the head. There's no way to emotionally prepare for that sight; nor is there a way to get over what you've seen. All you can do is put a protective shell around your heart and stay laser-focused on the job you're there to do. My first suicide completely shook me—a woman with her throat sliced open, hemorrhaging pools of scarlet. But after that one, they all mixed together as one enormous, horrific tragedy emblazoned in my memory. You have to numb yourself to the particulars, because remembering would render you catatonic, incapable of per-forming the task at hand. Forgetting becomes a gift.

Not long after I joined the CSI division, I was assigned to the police-involved shootings team, a group of officers who, with great pride and care, looked out for our fellow cops who risked their lives daily in the field.

AS A CRIME SCENE INVESTIGATOR, I worked the graveyard shift, from 10:30 p.m. to 6:30 a.m. Late one night in August 1988, our department received a call from dispatch. "Signal fifteen—officer needs assistance," said the operator. "We need all units at an apartment complex in Oak Cliff." Minutes later I and several other detectives arrived at the location.

The patrol cops had already cordoned off, with yellow police tape, the cement walkway where the incident had occurred. "What happened?" my sergeant asked one of the cops. When a pair of officers responded to a domestic violence call, the assailant, who was hiding in the bushes, had shot one cop, they explained; the other cop, fearing for his life, had run off into the complex's Laundromat. The wounded officer was en route to the hospital.

Using the tool kit and other equipment I always carried, I immediately began dusting for fingerprints, analyzing blood splatter, and searching for shell casings. You need a minimum of two hours to investigate a scene like that and sometimes far more. But fifteen minutes after I began photographing and dusting the long walkway leading up to the apartment where the incident had occurred, an object caught my eye. It was a pair of broken glasses splattered in blood. I leaned down and took a closer look at the spectacles. They looked exactly like a pair I'd seen before.

I stepped away and walked over to the sergeant. "Who did you say was shot?" I asked him. "Which officer?"

"It's someone by the name of Walter Williams," he told me.

I stared at him. "Did you say Walter Williams?" I said, hardly able to get the words out. My tongue felt glued to the back of my throat.

"Yes," confirmed the sergeant, who had no idea I knew him. "It was Walter Williams."

A chill spread through my body. "Which hospital did they take him to?" I asked.

"Methodist Dallas," he told me.

Without another word, I left my tools at the scene, jumped into a squad car, and drove myself to the nearby medical center. When I entered the waiting room, Joanne, Walter's wife, thrust herself into my arms and wailed. Through sobs, she told me that her husband had sustained a bullet injury to his head. He'd been rushed to the ICU, where he was battling for his life.

I entered his room and walked over to him. He lay there unconscious, hooked up to a beeping life-support machine. His breathing was labored. His head was wrapped in bandages stained in red. "Walter?" I said. *Silence*.

I sat down at his bedside, my body wracked with pain. The first thought that ran through my head was, *Man, this is why I never wanted you to be a field trainer*. From day one, I had worried that something horrible might happen to my best friend, but I had never imagined it would be as tragic as this. My second thought was one any officer would have: *This could have been me*.

A moment later Joanne entered the room with her eyes red, her head lowered. "Can you go to my house and take care of my kids?" she whispered. I nodded. As much as I wanted to stay right there with Walter, I knew his children needed me. Walter and Joanne had two teenagers and a ten-year-old son. When an officer arrived at their home in Irving to inform Joanne that her husband had been shot, he had escorted her to the hospital. She had learned of the seriousness of the injuries only once she arrived there. At a time before cellphones were ubiquitous, she hadn't called to update her kids. They were sitting at home and waiting, surrounded by the agony of unanswered questions.

Their eldest son, then about fifteen, answered the door when I arrived. Before I could utter a syllable, he cried out, "What happened to my daddy?" I stepped into the living room, where the other children were huddled together on the couch. An empty Kleenex box rested on the coffee table. No one spoke.

"We don't have all the details yet," I said, carefully measuring my words so as not to further alarm them. "Your father has been shot in the head, and he's still alive."

At that point, all three of the children descended into whimpers, the kind of primal grief that comes from a place beyond the soul. As I took a seat next to them on the couch, I didn't know what to say; no words can truly bring comfort at a time like that. Hours went by, and one by one, starting with the youngest, they drifted off to sleep. By three a.m., I was also out cold.

The ring of the house phone woke me. It was Joanne. "Brown," she said, "I don't know what to do."

"What do you mean?" I said. "What's happening?"

The doctors had told her that if they removed Walter from life support, he would almost surely pass. "I need to decide whether to take him off."

I paused. "If he's got a chance to make it," I told her, "you'll regret pulling the plug. I know they've only given him a small chance, but let the Lord make the decision for you. Don't you make it." She agreed, and we ended the call.

Fifteen minutes later she rang again. When she'd returned to Walter's room after our first call, she said, the nurses had told her he'd been spitting out his oxygen tube. They put it back in, and he spat it out again. That happened several times. By the time Joanne arrived back at her husband's bedside, he had taken his final breath at the age forty-seven. "I didn't have to make the decision," she told me through tears.

"Joanne, I'm so sorry." Even as I said those words, they felt inadequate. "Do you want me to wake up the kids and bring them to the hospital?" I asked.

"No, keep them with you," she said. "I'll be there soon." Soon after, an officer escorted her home, and I returned to the hospital. I wanted to see Walter one last time before the medical examiner took away his body. When I arrived at four a.m., all the officers Walter and I had gone through the academy with were there. We're a close-knit family.

I sat down next to Walter's lifeless body. "Walter," I whispered, as if he could hear me, "I can't do this without you, man." Tears welled up in my lids and spilled out onto my cheeks. All the emotion I'd been holding back came rushing forward. "This job ain't gonna be fun without you," I told him.

At twenty-seven, I'd never lost anyone close to me. I'd been constantly surrounded by tragedy, but somehow, even with such proximity to death, I'd always held it at a distance. It is only when grief strikes in your house, among those you cherish, in your family or on your force, that it becomes painfully personal. I knew Walter, a man of faith, was in heaven, but that realization didn't lessen the blow or quell the hurt.

That morning in Walter's hospital room, I made a choice in the quietness of my heart: I would leave the force. I'd find another job before quitting, so I could continue covering my bills, but the moment I did, I'd be out the door. I didn't care what the position was, as long as I didn't have to hurt the way I was hurting at my friend's bedside. Any job had to be better than this.

WHENEVER A COP HAS FALLEN in the line of duty, a companion officer is assigned to walk with the family through the burial and offer consolation. In the case of Walter's death, I was the chosen officer. As deeply as I was grieving, I set that aside so I could offer a strong shoulder for Joanne and the kids. They wept as Walter's casket was lowered into the ground. I did all my weeping later that evening at home, in private. I was utterly broken by my friend's loss and angry at God that He would allow it.

The week after the funeral I went to a Wednesday night prayer meeting. Since I'd started working graveyard, I'd been able to attend church only on and off. Oak Cliff Bible Fellowship was still my home, but on this particular evening, I visited Southern Crest Full Gospel Baptist, the church where a fellow crime scene investigator, the Reverend Frank Henderson, Jr., served as pastor. About a hundred congregants were gathered in the sanctuary. In the tradition of the Baptist church, members stood to testify during the service. During all my years in church, I'd never given a testimony. I made my way up to the microphone.

"I don't even know how to begin," I said, my voice cracking. I cleared my throat and started again. "My best friend was killed last week," I said. "I've been asking the Lord for comfort, but I don't feel any comfort. I've lost my hope, my faith, my trust. Walter was a good man who was trying to protect this city. I don't understand how God could allow a man like that to be shot in the head. What we're doing here every week, coming to church—it doesn't help. I don't know where to go from here. I want to hear what you-all have to say." Stone-faced, I stepped away from the mic and returned to my pew in the rear of the sanctuary.

One by one the members rose and came to the front. One woman wept as she told of the day, years earlier, when she'd lost her dear mother. An elderly man stood and shared how badly his heart had been broken when his wife and children were killed in an auto accident. Every person spoke of tragedy, of loss, of wanting to give up hope; some said their greatest heart-aches had driven them to their knees and ultimately back into the Savior's arms for solace. "I don't know why bad things happen to good people," one woman concluded, "and we may never know until we get to heaven. But we just have to keep trusting God. That is all we can do."

On another day, I might have been able to fully receive the words of encouragement I'd heard. This was not that day. Though I'd asked for insight, I hadn't really come to church to hear from others. I was there to confront God. I was there to ask Him why He'd allowed Walter's life to be cut so short in such a senseless act of violence. I wasn't trying to make peace with what happened; I'd walked through those church doors intending to withdraw the commitment I'd made years earlier in the rain. The words I'd spoken weren't a testimony; they were a farewell speech to the Lord. I was done.

The next day at work, I told my sergeant of my plans to resign and began putting in applications all over town. Just the thought of forging on without Walter was too heavy a burden for me to carry.

WHEN YOU'RE AS YOUNG as I was then, you think you're invincible. You live as though you have a guarantee of decades stretched out before you. You're focused only on the horizon, never on the sunset. If asked then, I would've denied feeling this way, but deep down I did. I'd come into the profession on a hero's errand, with a naïve sense of invulnerability. But the reality is that every one of us is frail. In a split second, the breath and strength and health that sustain us can, without warning, cease to be. When I lost Walter, it was the first time I'd stared that frailty in the face, and what I saw shook me to my core. It made me want to throw up my hands and give up not just on my profession but on my spiritual beliefs.

Southern Crest Baptist Church is the only reason I did not quit. I don't know why I returned there after that prayer meeting, but I did. And I stayed for several months. The people in that congregation held me up. They walked with me through my sorrow, my questions, and my inclination to turn my back on God. They took me by the hand and just would not let me go. In particular, a couple of deacons, as well as Reverend Henderson, stood with me. They literally prayed me back to my faith—as well as back onto the force.

CHAPTER 6

GROUND SHIFT

——

I MADE A DEAL WITH MYSELF IN TENTH GRADE. UP TO THEN, I'd been one of the best players on every sports team I'd joined. But soon after I enrolled in high school back in Oak Cliff, I, the kid who was always thinking ahead, began calculating my chances of going pro. Barry, a classmate who was a year behind me in school, was a phenomenal running back. As competitive as I was, I knew I didn't have his magic. I could win games all day long around Oak Cliff, but I wasn't going to make it to the NBA or the NFL. And yet athletics consumed me. When I wasn't studying, I was preparing for a game or playing one. *Is this the best use of my time?* I began thinking. *If I instead devote myself to academics, could I get into college, earn my degree, and go on to get a great job?*

By sixteen, I'd become more aware of my mother's financial struggles. I'd seen her even tearing up when she couldn't give us some of the small things we wanted. For all her valiant effort, we still hadn't been able to afford a home of our own or a car. Every mother wants her child to do better than she did, to build on the legacy she has put in place, and that is what my mother wanted for my brothers and me. She'd struggled every day to ensure our needs were met, and her example planted a seed in me. Following school, I wanted to become a strong provider for myself and, eventually, for my family.

So I decided to play the odds. I could make straight A's; I'd already proven that over many semesters. And since a pro career was clearly a long shot, I made an agreement with myself: I would set sports aside and focus solely on academics. In that arena, I could compete. I could stand out as the best. I could do what Mom had always urged us to do: aim to be productive with our lives. At the start of my sophomore year, I didn't go out for a single sports team.

Once I made that choice, everything shifted. Many of those who'd been my classmates back in second grade were no longer on the honors track; in our high school, you had to choose to take on the most challenging course work. In tenth and eleventh grades, I enrolled in every Advanced Placement class that was available. By twelfth grade, I'd completed all my AP courses and begun participating in a gifted and talented program my district offered. In it, those who'd finished all their AP course work could gain work experience by doing an apprenticeship in two career tracks. I was still planning to pursue law, so I spent my mornings in the office of attorney Larry W. Baraka and my afternoons at an engineering firm.

Larry was the first real-life lawyer I'd ever met. Then a newly minted attorney, he would go on to become the first black district judge in Dallas County. His presence alone was affirmation that someone who looked the way I did could be successful. While working for him, I could actually see myself completing law school and one day taking on court cases, the kinds of cases Perry Mason had once argued. I could visualize it.

In the office every day, Larry was as dapper as Perry had been: tailored suits, pressed white shirts and ties, creased pants. I, on the other hand, hadn't yet learned how to dress the part. I had some church clothes, but Mom didn't let me wear those to school. I didn't own a suit and tie. So I wore the casual clothes that most kids wore in the 1970s—big collars, bell-bottoms, platform shoes, bright colors—with an Afro to complete the look.

One day when we were scheduled to go to court, I dressed up more than usual. I chose a blue-plaid leisure suit, a second-hand one I'd once begged Mom to buy for me. Not only did it have huge buttons down the middle; it came with a short-sleeved coat, under which I wore a long-sleeved shirt. The night before, I'd even plaited my hair back to prepare it for a nice Afro. I just knew I was sharp.

That morning Larry took one look at me and directed me toward the back of the courtroom, where I took a seat. After the hearing, as we were on our way out, he whispered to me, "David, don't you ever wear anything like that again in court." He didn't elaborate. He just stated his admonition in a matter-of-fact way and moved on.

I thought, *What is he talking about? Is he joking?* Years later, I can see how I must have looked in that ridiculous getup, made worse by long sleeves under a short-sleeve suit and a giant Afro. But you could not have told me that I didn't look good. And as an aside, any of us who've ever worn leisure suits should have very little to say about the fashion choices of later generations. We have no room to talk.

Larry was not only a mentor for me but also a true friend. I could sense that he, like the many teachers who nurtured me along the way, wanted me to be successful. One such person was Miss Battle, my twelfth-grade government teacher. Her last name fit her: She was 100 percent no-nonsense, just like my mother. I didn't know it at the time, but she was just out of college and only twenty-two, only a few years older than her students. That year and for decades afterward, she stayed up to date on everything I did, saving every newspaper clipping. I know public schools get a bad rap, and sometimes for good reason. But the educators in my district really cared about me. Miss Battle. Coach Hulcy. My second-grade teacher. All were the Oak Cliff I knew.

WHEN I GRADUATED FROM South Oak Cliff High School in 1979, my classmates voted me Most Intellectual and Most Likely to Succeed. I voted myself most likely to move out of my mother's place. Mom had always made it clear that whatever I did, it could not involve lying around her apartment without a job. College was to be my passport to a new existence, a life on my own two feet. Because I was near the top of my class, I was offered a combination of scholarships and financial aid to attend a selection of state schools. That was a relief and a blessing, since my mother couldn't afford the cost of higher education. I was admitted to the University of Texas at Austin and enrolled there for the fall.

A week before I left for Austin, I attended a church across

the street from our apartment complex. The ministers there hosted a special Sunday service for the high school seniors going away to college. At the close of the gathering, they gave each of us a warm send-off, with hugs and congratulations. They also handed us a Bible, a medium-size King James Version. To this day, I still have that Bible.

THE MORNING OF MY DEPARTURE for UT Austin dawned bright and clear. My mother had, as usual, arisen at sunrise and helped me with last-minute packing. Both Mom and Mabel accompanied me to the Greyhound bus station. "You be good, son," my mother said, hugging me. Mabel handed me a meal she'd prepared for me. I thanked her, and we embraced. As I boarded the bus, the two most important women in my childhood stood outside and waited for me to pull off.

Once on board, I scanned the faces of those seated and searched for an open spot. There were several possibilities next to other black passengers, but for some reason, my attention landed on a white guy who looked like he was around my age. Remembering my improbable connection with Mike Shillingburg, I sat next to him and balanced my lunch box on my lap. He glanced at me and smiled.

"I'm David," I said.

"I'm Lance," he said.

Our connection was immediate; we talked for the duration of the bus ride. Lance, who'd come from a poor family just as I had, was also en route to UT Austin. We talked nonstop, traded stories of our high school years and application to college, as well as our excitement about living on campus and experiencing college. A couple hours into our conversation, I got hungry. I reached down, opened the lunch box Mabel had given me, and began devouring my food. Lance looked on in silence. Even when the bus came to a halt at a rest area where food was available, Lance didn't get off and purchase anything. I could tell he was hungry, and I figured he didn't have the money to buy himself a meal. So as much I wanted to savor every last bite of my food, I finally looked over at him and asked, "Would you like some?" He nodded yes— and in that instant, a meal meant for one became an opportunity to do for Lance what Mike Shillingburg had once done for me.

When we arrived in Austin, Lance and I waved goodbye and went our separate ways. On our large campus, I never saw him again. So the first day we'd met had also been our last—until decades later, in the most unexpected way, when our paths would cross again.

COLLEGE WAS AN ENTIRELY new world for me. UT Austin had only a smattering of black students, many of whom, like me, had come from poor families. Race is the yardstick by which diversity is often measured, but class, its twin sister, is also a gauge. When it came to the latter, I stood out like the inner city kid I was, in my cheap threads and generic sneakers. I was surrounded by students who drove BMWs and Mercedes to campus and sported designer clothing. By all outward appearances, it seemed we had little in common. Yet I knew better, in part because my earlier experiences had proven otherwise. My friendship with Mike and the year and a half I'd spent in San Francisco had taught me how to reach past race and class and any other superficiality and connect with others on a heart level. Though the early adjustment was challenging, I extended myself and eventually made friends with classmates, some of whom looked like me and many others who did not.

Where perceived dissimilarities exist, music can serve as a great equalizer. That was the case on our campus. As I entered my sophomore year in the fall of 1980, hip-hop was eclipsing R&B as the newest art form to capture the fascination of the young of all races. From the dorm rooms to the cafeteria to the parking lot, "Rapper's Delight" by the Sugarhill Gang played on a constant loop. Students of every background fell in love with the lyrics and beat. "Let's rock, you don't stop," rapped Wonder Mike. "Rock the rhythm that'll make your body rock!" By year's end, I'd heard the record so much I was sick of it.

Unlike nearly everyone I knew on campus, I mostly stuck with R&B. Michael Jackson had come of age with *Off the Wall*, and Teddy Pendergrass was turning out the lights with his love songs. The Commodores and Lionel Richie were easy like Sunday morning, Frankie Beverly and Maze were giving me happy feelings, and Sly and the Family Stone wanted me to stay. Lenny Williams would later sum up why I couldn't let go of R&B when he sang " 'Cause I Love You." And yet I couldn't hate on rap. I'm just old-school. That year on campus, rap was both entertainment and common ground.

When I arrived in Austin, I didn't declare a major right away. I still dreamed of becoming a criminal defense attorney, which meant I had my eye on law school—and I already knew I wouldn't be able to afford it. So I concocted a plan to complete my bachelor's degree, then take a job to put myself through law school. But there was a problem: Typical pre-law majors such as English, philosophy, and political science might not lead to a job that paid well enough to cover law school tuition. If I went down that road, I'd end up flat broke and in major debt. So rather than haphazardly choosing a course of study, I discussed my options with a college guidance counselor.

"How much does an English major earn right after college?" I asked, wanting to confirm my suspicions.

She stared at me as a grin spread across her face. "It depends on the job," she said. "But not much initially."

"What's the highest-paying major?" I asked. She shuffled through some papers on her desk and fished out a list of majors. After studying the list for a moment, she mentioned a few, including engineering, marketing, and computer science. "And accounting," she concluded. "That field tends to pay a good starting salary."

That was all I needed to hear. I knew nothing about accounting, but I was confident in my math skills. *I can do that,* I thought. *It's adding and subtracting and balance sheets.* It's far more than that, of course, but I had my gaze firmly affixed on the goal of a decent income. When you grow up in poverty, the practical takes precedence over the philosophical. I didn't have the luxury of traveling the world to "find myself" during my late teens and twenties. I just had to get through school and get on with a career. That same week I declared myself an accounting major and enrolled in the required courses.

One of my former high school buddies, David Lewis, the one who'd eventually work for Microsoft, made the same choice. He and I were roommates during our freshman year, and we'd both researched the starting salary of an accountant. It was approximately $21,000. That may not sound like a lot to some, but it was more than my mother had ever earned, except perhaps for those few years when she'd worked at Texas Instruments. Even with all her hours of overtime, her average annual income hovered around $17,000—enough to cover our basic expenses, but too little to purchase a home or a car, and certainly not enough to pay for a vacation. So $21,000 sounded like a jackpot to me.

As I sank into my studies—and began dating the woman I'd marry in 1982—from the outside looking in, the dramatic shift in my situation probably looked like an overwhelming flurry of events. In the space of a year and a half, I left home, transitioned to college, and stepped into family life—all while still a student. And yet I experienced the change not as an unsettling series of events but as an exciting new chapter filled with hope and anticipation. In my view, this is what it meant to grow into full manhood. My mother had done all the working in order to provide for my brothers and me. I'd never even worked a fast-food job while I was under her roof. Now, for the first time, it was my turn to take care of my family the way that she'd taken care of us.

Not long after I married, I landed a part-time job as a pizza deliveryman. My scholarships and financial aid were enough to cover my tuition, but I needed extra for rent and groceries. I worked as many hours as my supervisors would give me. The summer before, I'd scrounged up $750 in cash to buy a used '71 Buick Skylark. It was a gorgeous hunter green and didn't have many miles on it. Every evening at the start of my delivery route, I'd crank it up and make my rounds. Surprisingly, even while balancing thirty hours of work with a full-time course load, I didn't feel overwhelmed; that is youth's invaluable gift to each of us. It helped that my studies came fairly easily. I earned the same good grades I'd been earning since second grade. All seemed to be going well—and then I came home to Oak Cliff during the summer that changed everything.

THE EYES ARE WHAT I remember: dazed and empty, crimson and dilated, filled with a quiet rage. While I was home in Oak Cliff on that summer break in 1982, just after my sophomore year at UT Austin, the eyes I noticed belonged to an old high school classmate of mine, once known for his gregarious laugh and cheerful disposition. When he and I ran into each other near my mother's apartment, I almost didn't know him. He was nearly comatose.

"Hey, man, what's going on?" I asked him. He didn't speak. He didn't nod or smile. He didn't acknowledge my question. He just stared, as if he were looking through me rather than at me. There was no light in his eyes. He appeared, simultaneously, to be half-dead and capable of lunging forward to strangle me.

During my first week back in the neighborhood, I'd spotted that gaze all over town. Among the kids I'd once shot hoops with on the courts. Among those who'd gone through school with me. On street corners, in restaurants, in grocery stores.

"What's going on around here?" I finally asked a couple of my buddies who still seemed like themselves.

"These kids are trying crack cocaine," one friend explained. "It's all over the place."

"What does it do to you?"

"You try one hit, and you're hooked," he told me.

"You mean, like, totally addicted?" I asked.

"Yes," he said. "After a single smoke."

All I could think was, *But for the grace of God, that could have been me—one hit and hooked.*

I was stunned and horrified. A drug I'd never heard of had made Oak Cliff totally unrecognizable to me. Evidence of crack was everywhere: The lots where we'd played pickup basketball games sat empty, and the recreation centers had fallen strangely silent. In place of children playing tag and hopscotch until just before dusk, sellers lurked about, trading clear Baggies with small rocks of white powder. Gunshots rang out overnight, and on the news, drug-related shootings were reported frequently. While I'd been away, crack had transformed my neighborhood into a war zone. It looked as if a bomb had been dropped there. Oak Cliff was completely ravaged.

I stayed indoors for most of that summer. That's how utterly depressed and frightened I felt. By this time, Rickey had moved into his own apartment in Dallas and was putting himself through junior college. Kelvin, who'd graduated from high school and was working odd jobs while he figured out his next move, was still living at home. On one of the many long afternoons when I sat around Mom's apartment, heavy-hearted and trying to forget what was happening in Oak Cliff, I spotted it again. That look. Those eyes. That unsettling gaze. Right there in our living room, my own little brother was high on crack. I didn't say anything to Kelvin, because frankly I didn't know what to say. In our family, uncomfortable issues were seldom addressed head-on; it's just not the way we dealt with things. A wave of helplessness and anger swept over me. I had never felt so shaken.

While I'd return to college for one more year, my thoughts were never far from home—and soon I'd be back in Dallas for good.

CHAPTER 7

KELVIN

—

THE 911 CENTER IS THE DALLAS POLICE DEPARTMENT'S heartbeat, its epicenter. If anything goes wrong there, it can cost lives. Two years after I buried Walter but long before the ache of his loss dissipated, I passed the exam to become sergeant and was assigned to the 911 and Dispatch centers, both located in the basement of City Hall and right next to each other. Again, I was assigned to the graveyard shift.

I first managed only the 911 operators. All of them were civilians, and most were women, perhaps not coincidentally, since every female I've ever been close to, starting with my mother, has handled the greatest pressures with extraordinary calm. I'd been on the force for eight years, and until this job, I'd never supervised a team. I'm sure that had everything to do with my misguided approach to this new job: I came in with an authoritarian attitude, like some Clint Eastwood–type cowboy, handing out orders as if I already knew everything there was to know about the department. As a result, those women gave me pure hell. One busy Saturday evening, several of them disappeared from their stations, leaving only me and a few other operators to cover incoming calls. When I went racing around the floor to find them, they were enjoying a leisurely dinner. They did it to get my attention with a big lesson: *You rely on us as much as we rely on you.* And let me tell you, they gave me a crash course in how to supervise. How to get people to work hard for you by showing them how much you care. How to surrender your ego and allow others, even those you manage, to teach you. God has put many situations and people along my path for the purpose of humbling me. In 1991, He used those 911 operators.

A few months into my job, I began overseeing Dispatch in addition to 911—and I gained an even more sobering regard for just how critical that entire operation is to our department and our society at large. When an emergency call came in, a 911 operator answered, typed in the details of the situation, assigned it a priority from Levels 1 to 5, and forwarded it, via computer, to a team of dispatchers, who deployed officers to a given address. And what happened if a call was erroneously coded? That could be the difference between a homicide and a happy ending.

As the supervising sergeant on the floor, my job was to be sure that (a) Dispatch received complete information, particularly on high-priority calls and (b) my 911 and dispatch operators stayed fresh at their consoles. An exhausted clerk is prone to mistakes. The job is inherently stressful: For eight hours at a time, these operators hear from people in crisis and have to make split-second judgments about how best to help. If a call is appropriately coded as Priority 1, officers will turn on their sirens to get to an address. But if a tired operator, one who has been at her desk too long, erroneously codes a call as Priority 4—which means the cops will arrive in thirty minutes to an hour—that might be too late to save a life. Every step and misstep count.

And so does every spoken word. One evening in 1991, an officer became involved in a foot chase and subsequent fight with a suspect. The officer called in for backup. "What is your location now?" the dispatcher asked him. He told her the intersection he was closest to, but because he was so out of breath, she couldn't understand him. My team flew into action, rewinding the taped conversation to try to determine what the officer had said. None of us could make it out. Meanwhile, the dispatcher who'd taken the call deployed a police helicopter to search for the officer. The dispatchers and I feverishly continued rewinding that tape and listening to every second of it in slow motion, while we anxiously awaited any word from the copter pilot. After more than an hour, with our blood pressures through the roof, we finally received word of a miracle: The officer had been located. He even had the suspect in custody. The dispatcher who'd first received the call was so drenched in sweat and exhausted by the ordeal that she needed a half-hour break. Just another shift on the Dispatch desk—and an ordinary day in police work.

I'll be honest: As much as I came to enjoy my team members, many of whom are friends of mine to this day, I couldn't wait until that assignment was over. That's how intense the job was even for a relatively short period— eighteen months—so I can imagine how stressed the public servants are who field calls about society's darkest moments for years on end. Almost from the minute I got there, I was counting the days until I could get out of that division.

IN THE YEARS AFTER returning to Dallas to join the force, I saw my brother Kelvin only occasionally. It's not that Kelvin and I didn't want to connect; it's just that we'd both settled into our busy lives. After finishing high school, he was still trying to carve out a career path. In the meantime, he was working odd jobs around Oak Cliff. He still lived at home. When I'd stop by Mom's apartment to look in on her, he and I would sometimes catch up. We did so one evening in the spring of 1991.

"I'm thinking about becoming a truck driver," he told me.

"That's great," I told him. "Are you going to a truck-driving school?"

"I've already completed a program," he told me.

Though the idea of Kelvin driving long-distance, cross-country routes alone unnerved me, I didn't tell him I worried for his safety. I just did what older brothers often do: I kept my concerns to myself and wished him well. I wanted him to feel supported in his new venture. And I was pleased that he was taking some initiative. A few weeks after he'd told me of his plans, he landed work and began driving. He loved it from the first route.

In July 1991, a few months after I'd been assigned to the 911 Center and not long after Kelvin began driving, an office clerk came out onto the floor to find me.

"Your mother is on the office line," she told me.

"My mother?" I said. She nodded. My heart froze. Mom had never called me at work, and especially not after midnight. I rushed to the phone inside a nearby glass office and kept an eye on the Dispatch operation I'd been overseeing.

"Mom, what is it?" I said with no pause between each word. She did not answer. Instead, she began to weep.

"Tell me what's happening," I pressed. "What's wrong?"

"Kelvin was killed," she sobbed.

"What did you say?" My heart was hammering so fast in my chest that it felt as if it would tumble out onto the floor. The room grew dark and out of focus. My mouth went dry as cotton.

"What did you say, Mom?" I repeated, my voice quivering.

"David, your brother is dead," she declared.

My hand went limp. The receiver, one of those old beige rotary phones, slid from my palm and onto the ground. Two other sergeants, Frank and Jeff, noticed my reaction and came into the office. Jeff asked me what had happened. In shock, I heard myself explain that Kelvin was dead, although even as I spoke the words, I hadn't wrapped my brain around the reality of what I was saying. "I'm so sorry," they said over and over. With the receiver still lying on the floor, I darted from the office and out toward the parking lot. Jeff and Frank followed me. They insisted on driving me to my mother's apartment to ensure I didn't get into a wreck on the way there.

Mom met me at the door, her face strewn with tears. She threw herself into my embrace, and together we stood and wept. Moments later, when my mother's wailing temporarily subsided, I posed a question, one I would later regret. "Mom," I asked her, "are we going to see Kelvin in heaven?"

She stared at me in disbelief. I will never forget the sternness in her eyes, the sober look that spread across her face. "We can trust in the Lord that we will," she said clearly, without a single crack in her voice. "And don't you ever doubt God again, son."

The moment I learned Kelvin was deceased, I'd assumed he'd done something wrong to cause his death, and so his place in heaven would be revoked. My mother took my question for what it was—a sign that I was doubting God's promise to hold tightly to His children's hands and guide them into paradise. "I'm so sorry I said that," I told my mom, hugging her again. "Please forgive me." I'd been in no position to judge; only the Father can do that.

I maintained that perspective as the details of Kelvin's death came to light. My brother had been driving through the Southwest and stopped in Phoenix. There he found a dealer and purchased crack cocaine. After smoking it, he concluded the drug was fake because he hadn't gotten the high he was expecting. He returned to the dealer and demanded that he receive either a refund or a real drug. When the dealer refused, a fight ensued. During that argument, the dealer shot and killed Kelvin. My brother was only twenty-eight.

The incident had happened two days earlier. But since Kelvin didn't have my mom's number on him, it had taken some time for the authorities to locate the next of kin. To this day, I don't know all the details surrounding his death. I could have called the Phoenix Police Department and inquired, but I had no desire to hear more. It wouldn't bring Kelvin back or ease the crushing blow of his loss.

Looking back on the years leading up to my brother's death, I can see that he must have been caught in the clutches of crack's powerful grip. Before the epidemic hit the streets of Oak Cliff, I'd thankfully already gone away to college. Kelvin and his friends weren't so fortunate. As the neighborhood changed and crack became readily available, that environment became my brother's new normal. And yet in many ways, we were no different from each other. He took one hit of a drug he'd never heard of and became addicted. I took one puff of a cigarette that, in a later era, could have been crack. Same behavior, different outcome. I'm no different. I'm no better than anyone.

Even after that pivot-point summer drawing me back to our neighborhood to fight the crack epidemic, Kelvin and I had never discussed the dazed look I'd noticed in his eyes. And as time went on, I didn't feel the need to bring it up. As a beat cop, when I'd been arresting drug users on every street corner and closing down crack houses by the dozen, I hadn't run across my brother. I also hadn't ever again witnessed him high. I believed he'd gotten clean. That was what I told myself. As hard as I was on the scores of drug users and dealers I locked up, I couldn't face that my own family, my own brother, might be among them.

My mother might have suspected Kelvin was struggling, but she didn't discuss it with him either. Every family has a culture, a way of handling difficult subjects, and in our family, we fall silent and take it for granted that we're on the same page. We then hope and pray, all the while continuing to think only the best of our loved one. That had been my mother's approach with Kelvin, as well as with anyone in our extended family who'd shown frailty. Without question or condemnation, without even the slightest hint of criticism in her eyes, my mother always embraced those closest to her. She still does. That is the nature of a loving mom. In her presence, there is no space for castigation. Even amid the heartbreaking circumstances of her child's death, she did not question whether Kelvin would live on in eternity. She still trusts that her baby is now resting in the Father's arms.

That week my brother's body was transported to Dallas. I asked Reverend Frank Henderson, the minister who'd helped me get through Walter's death, to give the eulogy at Kelvin's funeral. He preached the sermon of his life. As I sat there in the front pew next to Mom, both of us clad in black with our heads hung as low as our spirits, I buried my face in my palms and cried. For three years, I'd been slowly healing from the devastation of losing Walter; Kelvin's death reopened the wound. The pastor must have sensed what my family and I needed to hear. He shared the story of how Mary wept upon hearing of Lazarus's death. "As overcome with emotion as she was," he told the congregation, "she had to release Lazarus. She had let him go, Jesus declared. She had to place him in God's hands."

When you lose a family member in the manner in which we lost Kelvin, it's beyond difficult to accept. You can't really even believe it's true. You look back, with great regret, on all the things you did or didn't do, words you could have spoken, things you wish you could say now. That sermon helped my family begin to grapple with our grief, to release Kelvin and set aside the heartache surrounding how he died.

You don't ever really get over the loss of a loved one. I'd learned that in the years following Walter's death, and I learned it again now, as I grieved for Kelvin. In your sadness, you just keep getting up every day, breathing your way from one moment to the next. Time doesn't heal; it merely dulls the pain and, years later, at last dims your memory of it.

If tragedy has a silver lining, it's that it serves as preparation, particularly in a field like mine in which death is a constant. When others are inconsolable, I know what to say and what not to say. In some cases, you can tell someone to have faith. To hold on. To trust in God's plan. In many other cases, you should be altogether silent. Because more than any words, your presence is itself an antidote.

I CARRIED ON WITH my work in the 911 Center, grateful for something to keep me occupied. In a sense, the constant flow of emergencies, of lives hanging in the balance, puts your grief in perspective. We are all bound together by loss, by frailty. Today it's my loss. Tomorrow it will be yours. None of us gets through life without confronting sorrow.

Walter and I had promised each other that we'd push ourselves forward, constantly reach for the next highest rung on the ladder. So as my time in the 911 Center drew to a close, I began looking for my next assignment. I called around to various divisions. I could not find an opening. A few days before my eighteen months were complete, I ran into Captain Doug Kowalski, a Northeastern guy who'd moved south years earlier, in the break room.

"Dave, how's it going?" he asked in his New York accent.

"Man, I'm trying to get out of nine-one-one," I told him.

"Where are you trying to go?" he said.

"Anywhere," I said with a chuckle.

"We're giving a SWAT sergeant test tomorrow," he said. "Could you be ready?"

"You'd better believe I can be ready," I said. I'd always admired SWAT—the special weapons and tactics team that is the most highly competitive and physically rigorous in all of policing.

At nine the next morning, I took and passed the physical fitness exam; there's also an interview, but since Doug vouched for me, I did not have to take it. Two weeks later, during the next payroll cycle, I transferred to SWAT. It still amazes me that one serendipitous conversation began the next seven years of my path. By then, I knew all too well that a single interaction could alter one's journey. Mike Shillingburg had taught me that in sixth grade.

CHAPTER 8

ARIZONA AVENUE

———

A SUCCESSFUL DRUG RAID BEGINS NOT WITH A WEAPON but with a strategy. As a SWAT sergeant and squad leader, I'd huddle with my team of eight and map out every detail of an impending operation: the home location, the clandestine approach, the best point of entry. The slammer, a squad officer holding a seventy-pound slab of iron, always moves in first and crashes the door for the six other officers to charge in with pistols drawn: two to the left, two to the right, and the sergeant, toting the only machine gun, down the middle to play cleanup and return fire. It was all about controlling the situation, clean and quick, while minimizing the use of force. That was the plan when my squad rolled up to a drug house on Arizona Avenue in south Oak Cliff one Friday afternoon in 1993. The dealers there had set up a one-stop shop for dope of every variety: crack, weed, heroin, LSD. We were going to shut these guys down.

Our van pulled up a few doors down from the address. The eight members of our sister squad, a backup team, had secretly staked out their places at various points around the home's perimeter. With hardly a sound, we filed quickly from the van and into our positions behind the slammer. As we approached the porch, a slew of bullets sprayed out from a front window and hit the slammer and another squad officer. The bullets lodged into the slammer's Kevlar ballistic vest, the sheer force temporarily knocking him to his knees. The other officer was struck in the extended Kevlar protector that covered his groin. Both collapsed to the ground as we all released several rounds of cover fire.

Two cops moved right into the path of the gunfire, stepping over their teammates' bodies, as others of us retreated temporarily to call for an ambulance to tend to our wounded officers. A minute later we all advanced directly toward the shooter. A series of bullets swooshed by my ear, narrowly missing my skull. I could feel my body shifting into sensory overload, giving me heightened perception and an expanded, seemingly superhuman view of my surroundings. I quickly recovered to discharge my weapon, but the shot did not take down the gunman, who continued firing.

I was in survival mode, just trying to stay alive. My face was covered in perspiration; I could feel the blood coursing through my veins. As my heart hammered away with a singular force, it felt as large as my entire chest. As loud as the gunfire was, the scene felt eerily silent.

Meanwhile a second guy, perched at the window and leaning out, targeted the other squad members, whose pistols were no match for his MAC-11 with clips that could hold several rounds. Just as I'd practiced so many times during training, I did a quick magazine change, enabling me to continue firing from my trusted fixed-stock MP-5 Heckler & Koch machine pistol in fully automatic mode on the widest aperture. As I reloaded my long banana clip, the guys in the house kept shooting at us.

Moments later, Scott McDonald, our sister squad's sergeant and the best SWAT team leader on the planet, leaned out from a tree behind which he'd been staked and, with laser focus amid the chaos, killed the first dealer with a single shot to his head. My other squad members then charged in as Scott and I laid down more cover fire aimed at the second shooter. As we entered the house, no one knew what to expect.

THE EXTRAORDINARY FORETHOUGHT THAT went into our drug raids began with an undercover narcotics officer. Days before the raid, a detective would be sent in to make several dope buys while surveilling every inch of a building's interior and exterior. Once a judge signed a warrant, we had three days to pounce.

Long before we put on our forty-pound ballistic vests, we answered every question there was to ask about the property and its inhabitants: What time of day is business most brisk? Are there toys in the yard that might indicate the presence of children? Is there an alleyway at the back of the home? Are there doors inside that are barricaded, and if so, which ones?

In the case of the Arizona Avenue shooting, the detective had noticed the assault weapons the dealers possessed, which was why we had two SWAT teams and why I carried extra machine guns and magazines. At times investigators even identified the "good eye"—a person, usually a local kid, hired by the drug dealer to monitor the situation on the street outside the house. The good eye might seem to just be chilling on his front porch, minding his own business. But he was on the lookout for cops so he could hastily alert the dealer as they approached.

Whenever my team loaded into our van ahead of an operation, we'd initially blow off steam by joking around, playing the dozens, and so on. But all laughter ended when the driver yelled, "Five minutes out!" At that point, I, the leader, would repeat every step of our plan. Two minutes before game time, I'd say, "Lock and load—safety off!" I'd then look each of the seven officers in the eyes, one by one, and remind them of their role. "After you break down the door," I'd tell the slammer, "I want you to step to the right and let us pass you, then drop your slammer and draw your pistol to take up the rear." Repeat, repeat, repeat—you do a lot of that as a SWAT sergeant. During a crisis, when the fight-or-flight impulse arises, that instinct is so strong that muscle memory kicks in. You have to battle against doing your own thing. I've seen slammers knock out a door and then just stand there, frozen in fear. That's why repetition is so critical. Before each officer steps out of that van, your instructions should be the last thing they hear.

You never ride to a scene in exactly the same way; that would become predictable. We constantly change our approach just to keep the suspects guessing, to stay one step ahead of them at all times. In some cases, we'd park several blocks away, near the command post van, and arrive at the address by foot; other times our driver would screech right up to the front of the drug house and we'd burst through the door so quickly that the occupants had no time to scatter. In many cases, we'd arrive through a back alley or an adjacent backyard at three a.m. When it comes to an operation's success, the element of surprise is paramount.

Each of our steps was measured. A maneuver called a duck walk—carefully placing your foot down, heel to toe—allowed us to remain stable and flat-footed enough to return fire if a crisis arose. Incidentally, athletes use the same tactic because being in balance allows you to throw stronger passes or make a more accurate basketball or golf shot. As we made our approach, we staggered ourselves intentionally. If a cop off to the right got shot, for instance, the cop behind him and slightly to his left could likely avoid a bullet and even return fire. In SWAT, a queue isn't just a queue; it's a line of defense.

The preservation of life, both ours and others', is the priority in our training. Will we pull the trigger on a gunman who refuses to surrender? Absolutely. Will we take down a criminal who fires at us first? Absolutely we will, since there's not a cop on the force who doesn't want to make it out alive. If a suspect shoots at a cop first and he or she returns fire, that's not a movie I want to see; it's a setup for a police funeral. That's precisely why SWAT officers are trained to fire their weapons only as a last resort but without hesitation.

THERE WAS A MENTALITY that went along with SWAT: In order to sustain the intensity of the work, you had to believe you're the best. On my squad, we were always pushing ourselves to outdo not only one another but also the seven other teams that existed in the Dallas PD then. You had to be determined to stay on top, in shape, at the ready when a crisis popped up. That was what drove us to work so hard.

That work was unrelenting. Following the initial training that every squad officer completed, we constantly practiced our assigned specialties. For instance, one squad member was always the rifle shot. I strove to become the expert marksman on my team, so I spent a lot of time at the shooting range, perfecting my skills so that, during a shootout, my training would take over. Carrying out your task on the squad was about more than just preparing; it was about living on alert and staying sharp. We weren't called upon every day, but during the 100 to 150 times a year when we were, we had to be ready for the specific situations our department handled—barricaded persons (a hostage, for instance, or a suspect who would not come out), drug busts, and crowd control at protests and beyond. A SWAT team is a standing army.

Mornings always followed the same routine. We reported to work at the patrol station in downtown Dallas, a location central enough to allow us to quickly deploy to any address. Unless a crisis emerged, most days began with rigorous weight lifting and cardio. SWAT officers, whose body fat percentage and physical abilities are tested every six months, have to stay in top shape. Fail the exam? You're out and back to routine patrol work. I've never had a natural six-pack, so I had to watch my diet in order to maintain a lean stomach. I ate plenty of protein, tuna in particular, and no breads or sweets. I didn't miss those foods. The intense pressure to stay in top shape made it easier to stick to a strict diet than it might otherwise have been.

Our after-lunch training schedule rotated daily. Sometimes

we'd go to a vacant home and practice door slamming and entry for hours on end. Other times, at the range, I'd fold up a twenty-dollar bill and announce, "Whoever gets closest to hitting this bill wins the cash." Some weeks we'd rehearse our method for taking a blind corner, a serious drill. If one team member put himself in a poor tactical position in the real world, the other seven knew they'd have to put themselves in the line of fire to save that fellow cop. "You've got to do better on your blind corners," we'd often remind one another. Our squad was only as strong as our weakest cop, and we competed to maximize one another's performance. As was true during that gun battle on Arizona Avenue, our lives depended on each team member's performance.

Before that raid, I'd chased and fought with plenty of criminals, but I'd never been shot at. In fact, when I initially heard the sound, I stopped and looked around, like, *Who's playing with fireworks?* Firing a weapon on a range is one thing; being in a gunfight is an entirely different experience. You can't re-create a life-or-death situation in target practice. You do your best to be ready, yes, but there's no foolproof preparation for the adrenaline surge that takes over your body when a bullet whooshes by your head.

THE GOOD EYE HAD done his job. Our detective hadn't been able to identify an informant in advance of the operation, and unbeknownst to us as we approached the house, the kid had warned the dealers. That's why they'd started shooting as we approached through the door.

I don't know how we made it out of that gun battle alive.

Terry Cahill, Joe Chatham, Charlie Tubbs, Tony Black, Sam LaPierre, Stan Bass, Greg Lowe, Joe Maines, Billy Ailey, Bobby Favors, Brian Verdine, and Mark Paghi are the bravest, most courageous, and most ethical men I know. They are my brothers for life.

Following the shootout, the first assailant, a young man of about seventeen, lay dying in his own blood after taking that bullet to his head. The second gunman, sixteen, had gunshot wounds to his abdomen. We eventually filled the house with tear gas, then threw in stun grenades. When we entered, blood was splattered all over the living room amid dozens of small clear Baggies of crack cocaine.

A slew of backup officers and an ambulance came screaming across town with full sirens toward our location. From their nearby van, our command post team, including the undercover narcotics officer, had called 911 as soon as the operation went to hell. Scott and I instructed officers to put handcuffs on the second gunman before an EMT carried him away. During a sweep of the home, two other teens were discovered. The first gunman was pronounced dead.

Later, as a detective took down my report, he asked me, "How many shots did you fire?" "I don't really know," I stammered, still dazed from the trauma of what I'd just experienced. "Maybe about ten." Despite planning out every detail of the operation beforehand, I couldn't recall basic information such as the location address or how we'd approached the door. That's what trauma can do to your brain, particularly when you've never previously been shot at. Thank God I'd had an experienced squad. I'd later learn that I'd reloaded my magazine multiple times and fired more than fifty rounds. In total, two hundred rounds were fired during that gun battle. Our response had been automatic. The hundreds of hours we'd spent in training had taken over.

AROUND SWAT, THAT DRUG RAID became known as the Arizona Avenue shooting—and it was a significant turning point in our use of weaponry and body shields. It was also the start of the militarization of policing in our department. From then on, all squad team members carried fully automatic machine guns— Heckler & Koch nine-millimeter MP5s or AR-15s—and wore ballistic helmets made of Kevlar. They'd had neither before that raid, since only the squad leader and sergeant carried a machine gun. And the pistols my team carried didn't do jack against the kind of gun power those dealers had. As bullets pierced the air by our guys' heads, they'd been wearing baseball caps. Not good enough when someone is trying to kill you. That incident changed the game.

In the coming years on SWAT, I would experience more than my share of shootouts and drug raids. My ascent through the ranks of the department coincided with the epidemics of crack- and drug-related violence that had drawn me into law enforcement in the first place—so for me, the work was satisfying even though it was dangerous. During one particularly hazardous operation, my team and I were called upon to serve a drug warrant on an apartment in South Dallas. Around our department, we'd given the building a nickname: New Jack City. As in that 1991 crime drama—where Scotty Appleton (played by Ice-T) is an undercover cop in pursuit of drug kingpin Nino Brown (played by Wesley Snipes) who has taken over a Harlem,

New York, building to run a thriving crack business—our New Jack City was a complex in which just about every resident was somehow involved in peddling drugs.

We planned to target the heart of the operation—the apartment where the dealers kept most of their drugs, money, and weapons. In advance, as in every operation, our undercover officers identified the location where the stash was kept and surveilled the peak hours of drug buying. Once it began, our slammer busted down the door, and we filed into the living room. There, on a long couch facing away from the door, ten young black men sat smoking reefer in front of a large television screen. You won't believe what they were watching—*New Jack City*. In the scene that was playing, the SWAT officers were serving up warrants inside the complex.

"Put up your hands!" I shouted. Dazed and befuddled, they all stumbled to their feet, staring at the screen, then back at us officers. I'm sure they were thinking, *Is this really happening or is this reefer making me hallucinate?* We were dressed exactly like the SWAT team in the movie—all black, in big vests and fatigues—and carrying machine guns. Before they could move or reach for their weapons on the nearby coffee table, we were on top of them. We put them in handcuffs and guarded them in the living room as the narcotics agents came in to sweep the place for drugs. The movie played on. When it got to the scene in which Nino Brown and his buddies take down some SWAT agents, one of my team members glanced over at the guys. "Well," he said with a smirk, "I guess you can't believe everything you see on TV."

I've never seen a group of dealers looking more pissed. Tens of thousands of dollars in crack was seized that day.

Back in the 1990s, it was productive to run warrants the way we did—during peak times, when the dealers were likely to be on hand with large amount of dope and cash. Today's drug houses are smaller as the dealers have gotten smarter. They keep only as much dope on hand as they know they'll sell in a four-hour period; they hide the rest in what is known as a stash house, at a separate location. Which means that nowadays when cops raid, they're ruining that dealer's business only for that four-hour time period. And as soon as the coast is clear and one or two dealers are taken into custody, the other dealers on their team can go right back to selling, sometimes even in the same house.

Minus the murder and the mayhem, the drug business is not much different from any lawful, well-run enterprise. If those young dealers had applied their instinctual entrepreneurial savvy to legal businesses in their neighborhoods, those communities might have been transformed for the better. Instead of destroying the lives of people who looked like them, they could have provided decent grocery stores, home-remodeling shops, safe entertainment venues and attractions for families, elder care and transportation for seniors. *Quit killing us and then blaming someone else,* I've often thought. Imagine what the 'hood would look like if dope dealers and hustlers became legitimate inventors, venture capitalists, and business moguls.

ARIZONA AVENUE WASN'T ONLY the first time I'd been shot at; it was also the first time I'd been with a group of officers who actually killed someone. And to tell you the truth, as much as I wish none of those kids had to be killed or wounded, I was glad it was us who'd survived. If they'd had their way, I would've been burying one of my squad members the way I once buried Walter. I also would have critiqued myself so harshly that I would have no longer been able to do my job. A traumatic incident like that doesn't end when the shooting stops. For days and weeks, you relive it. You dream about it. You imagine how things would have turned out differently if you'd leaned left rather than right.

In the following years, I'd learn what some of my experienced squad members already knew: With every gun battle, your reaction time changes. You still have the same physiological responses, but they slow down. You're able to think more clearly, control your reflexes, and make smarter decisions. My training on the range also shifted after I was shot at. I took my time. I was more focused and accurate. I was slow, methodical, and careful. The whole time I was thinking about that bullet whizzing by my head—and preparing myself for the next time it might happen.

CHAPTER 9

THE GOOD FIGHT

D.J. WAS ELEVEN THE YEAR PRESIDENT BILL CLINTON VIS-
ited Dallas. By then, my son's mother and I had divorced, and we shared joint custody, which meant I relished my precious weekend time with him. One Sunday over breakfast, I told D.J. about an upcoming assignment I'd been given. As a SWAT sergeant, I'd be part of the dignitary protection team to host the president and the first lady.

"Will you get to meet them?" D.J. asked with eagerness in his voice. Even when he'd been much smaller, he had a wide-eyed curiosity and excitement about my work.

"Yes, I'll get to meet them," I said. I'd been looking forward to the day. There's a majesty to the office of the presidency, a power and grandeur that transcends the person who holds the position. You can't see Air Force One land or step into the White House without feeling a profound sense of our shared history as Americans.

"Dad, could I come?" my son asked me. I told him that wouldn't be possible. It's extremely rare for the children of officers to accompany their parents to work, particularly for such a high-profile occasion. But the following week, without mentioning anything to D.J. so as not to raise his hopes, I put in a request. To this day, I don't know what I said to convince my supervisor to allow me to bring my son onto the tarmac as the president and first lady departed, but he agreed. D.J., of course, was over the moon.

My son and I, along with the local officials and members of the media who had formed a line in anticipation of the president's departure, stood near the stairway entrance of Air Force One. The president and the first lady arrived in their motorcade, and when the car door opened, they emerged near the stairway. D.J. and I could not have been smiling more broadly.

One by one each person in line stepped forward to greet the first couple. After the president shook D.J.'s hand, Hillary stooped down to D.J.'s height, took him by the hand, and said, "Hello there!" Then quite unexpectedly, she stepped off to the side with D.J. and began a one-on-one conversation. The other squad members' expressions told me what they must have been thinking: *Does the first lady know you?* She did not, of course. As I stood there, I was asking myself, *What could they be talking about?* Believe me, I strained hard to hear, but I couldn't make out a single word of what they were discussing. Yet by the wide grins they both wore, I could tell they'd hit it off.

"May I take your son onto Air Force One for a tour?" the first lady asked me. "Uh, yes, ma'am—sure," I stammered, astounded at the offer. "Follow me," she said. My son glanced in my direction, and once I gave him the nod of approval, he followed Hillary up the stairs. Fifteen minutes later they returned. She hugged D.J. and they waved goodbye. As they parted, the White House photographer snapped a picture of the two shaking hands for a final time.

That evening when we arrived home, my son told me about his private tour. He was amazed by how large the plane's interior had seemed. "So what did you and the first lady talk about?" I asked him. A smile spread across his face. "That's between me and the first lady," he declared. I never did find out the details of their conversation, but I do know the whole experience was one that D.J. cherished. And for me, his father, it was a proud moment that I was delighted to share with my son, most of all because being singled out made him feel like the most special child in the world. The picture still hangs on my wall.

IN 1995, MY SQUAD had an open position: countersniper, the person who specialized in shooting a powerful long-distance rifle, such as the .308 bolt-action Winchester we used back in the day. There are two countersnipers on each team because if a sniper attacks, you want to be able to triangulate the gunman and return fire from more than one direction. To fill the vacancy, I wanted to choose someone who, in addition to passing the physical test and becoming an excellent shot, would be a good personality fit for our group. There are some big egos on SWAT, and a newbie needs to be able to come in and be a team player. Up to then, every countersniper in the history of the department had been a man. I, always a bit of a maverick, wanted a woman. I never forgot how hard my mother had worked in raising me, and how difficult some of her employers had made her job. Ever since I'd supervised that smart group of women in 911 and Dispatch, I'd been on the lookout for ways to promote female officers. It was my way of paying it forward.

My gender preference had to do with more than that, though. I did my research and discovered that women happen to be among the best rifle shots in the world. In the Olympics, target shooting is a sport that women excel at—and yet very few women even applied to SWAT. Before casting a net, I thought about it long and hard. I knew if I selected a woman, she had to be better than good, or else the men would give her a hard time and try to run her off. I started asking around: "Do you know any female officer who's a great shot and can pass the SWAT test?" A few names surfaced. Anita Dickason's rose to the top.

Anita was in extraordinary physical shape, and she was a superior pistol shooter. However, she'd have to learn how to fire a rifle. I was confident she could do so. For one thing, she was strong-willed and stubborn as hell. During my interview, for instance, a few other SWAT team members and I asked her some tough questions about how she'd handle certain scenarios. "If a commander who has information you aren't privy to ordered you to shoot and kill a suspect, would you do it, no questions asked?" Without hesitation, she confirmed that she would. Any other answer would have been unacceptable because countersnipers have to rely on their commanders to make the tough decisions in order to save lives; such orders are time sensitive and not up for debate.

I brought her on for a trial period. At the time, Tony Black was the other countersniper on my team. I knew if I chose Anita, he'd be the kind of guy who'd give her a fair shot. I also knew, given his skill level, he'd make a great teacher for her. I pulled Tony aside. "Don't cut her any slack," I told him. "We've got to be able to put our lives in her hands."

Anita did her training on the shooting range. At various times, to test her progress, I'd simulate a real gunfight by pulling up to a scene and saying "Get down on your rifle, and let's see what you've got." It took her an eternity to get proned (down on her stomach), to aim, and then to actually fire. "If you move that slow during an operation," I told her, "somebody will be burying me." She improved her speed, and after a couple months, she could quickly and accurately shoot a target from three hundred yards away. In fact, she became so great that she began taking part in competitive shooting outside work. "Now you're ready," I told her. "Now I'm willing to put my life in your hands."

With great pride, I officially offered her the countersniper position on our squad. During my remaining years on SWAT, she proved she could do everything the men could, and sometimes even better. If some fool was crazy enough to take aim at us during a raid, they'd soon discover that Anita did not play. That woman took care of business.

OVER THE COURSE OF many raids, my squad cemented its reputation as one of the best. Amid the fierce competition that exists among SWAT teams, we'd proved ourselves. And not just on that crack raid. Time and again we were called upon to resolve some of the most dangerous situations, particularly by using gunfire, though only as a last resort. In one barricaded-person case, Dispatch called us to the home of a mentally ill man who was holding his own children hostage; he and his former wife were entangled in an acrimonious custody dispute. The patrol cops and negotiators had spent hours trying to bargain with this guy, who was white and middle-aged. He eventually let his children leave the home—but he refused to come out himself. Through his front windows, officers could see him wildly swinging a machete.

I knew we had to proceed with caution; a peaceful resolution is always our goal. And yet I also knew we might ultimately have to use force, because there are few other ways to take control of someone who's brandishing a sword and lunging toward you. "We're going to launch a canister of tear gas in there before we enter," I told my team. I thought that would disorient the man long enough to give us a tactical advantage that would allow us to take him down without gunfire. Well, that approach didn't work at all. In fact, once the smoke bomb filled his living room, he became even more agitated and swung the machete with greater intensity. It was the first time I'd ever seen such a reaction. When most people are teargassed, they rub their eyes and fall to the ground. Not this man. So I moved on to another idea: We threw in a flash bang, a nonexplosive stun device designed to startle anyone in its proximity. There is a risk that a flash bang can start a fire, but in this case, the benefit outweighed that risk. The plan worked to perfection. Seconds after we hurled the device, we stormed through the door and wrestled the man to the ground before he could take a swing. No gunfire was necessary. We handcuffed him, and he was transferred to a mental health facility.

As our squad became known for its strong tactical skills, we were sometimes called in on our off days. That's what happened one Sunday night in 1994, when my supervisor rang me at home. "Please get your team over here to help us locate two armed and violent barricaded persons," she said. Earlier that evening a couple of young guys had gone on a robbery spree in downtown Dallas: They'd hijacked a car and robbed several shop owners at gunpoint, fleeing with bags of cash. When patrol cops had arrived on the scene, they'd chased the men on foot, but in the end, the suspects had eluded them. They'd disappeared somewhere onto the property of a random home in a nearby residential area. Residents of the home were promptly evacuated as officers searched the premises. The SWAT squad on duty was called to the scene but could not find them anywhere. That was when we were brought in. "The patrol cops are convinced they're in there somewhere," my supervisor told me.

I rang each of my squad members. "Why are we being called in on our day off?" they all asked. "Because you're the best," I told them. Not only did I believe that was true; my time as 911 supervisor had shown me that managing your people involves reassuring them of their skills. That's what can often bring out the best in a person. And of course, when you're asking someone to get off the couch on a Sunday evening after watching hours of football, a little ego stroking is never a bad idea.

Our initial search of the home, a large old house, yielded no results. "Does this place have an attic?" I asked the patrol cop. It did—and it had already been scoured. I then walked around the home's perimeter, considering every possibility of where these men could be hiding. I noticed the house was slightly elevated, by about two and a half feet, on a pier and beam foundation. When I circled back to the front of the home and spotted, at the base of the porch, an entrance about the size of a doggie door, I asked the officer, "Does this home have a crawl space?" No one had checked. "We've gotta go in and search underneath this house," I told my team. We came up with a plan, based on the layout of the home's upper floors, of how we'd search the crawl space. Five of us would go in—two to the left, two to the right, and me down the middle. Anita Dickason, my countersniper, was among us.

The slammer kicked down the door. But when we tried to squeeze through the entrance wearing our Kevlar helmets and two ballistic vests, we couldn't fit. So despite the risk to our lives—these suspects were armed and had robbed at gunpoint—we abandoned our helmets and large outer vests. Even after we'd stripped down, the entrance was barely large enough for us to slither through. But one at a time, on our hands and knees and with our guns and flashlights at the ready, we did. The slammer and another squad member remained outside as our backup crew.

The space was pitch-black and filthy. It reeked of urine. We could hear rats skittering around as we entered. In the dark, we slithered along the grime on our bellies, feeling the cobwebs hanging down into our faces. We slid our way through the first half of the base and found no one. Then, at the back right rear, my eyes having adjusted somewhat to the darkness, I noticed a blind corner. I motioned to the officer nearest the corner and mouthed to him, "Can you see back there?" He could not; nor could any of the rest of us. I knew the gunmen had to be back there. "If you don't come out," I yelled, "we're going to start shooting!" *Crickets.*

"I'm giving you until the count of three to show your faces," I bluffed. "One! Two! Three." *Not a peep.* In certain barricaded-person situations, our officers and negotiators spend hours playing good cop in order to apprehend a suspect. But you can't negotiate with two fools on a violent robbery spree. You've got to be the bad cop and get tough immediately. "You guys better come out here before we blow your heads off!" I hollered, even louder than before. Seconds later a pair of hands appeared around the corner, waving in surrender. One down, one to go.

Anita and another officer grabbed the man and dragged him through the muck. At the door, the slammer handcuffed him. Meanwhile I began threatening suspect number two, who was still pretending not to be down there. "Your friend was a son of a gun," I yelled, "and you're a *stupid* son of a gun! We're getting ready to shoot you and leave you under this house to rot, and ain't nobody down here to even witness it." I had no intention of shooting the guy, but I had to make him think I would. It worked. After a few more threats, he at last gave himself up. But then as we tried to pull him out, he resisted by making his whole body go limp. We dragged his butt out anyhow.

Our search team then went in and combed every crack and crevice of that crawl space. Around that blind corner, they found the men's two guns and an enormous bag of stolen cash.

IN ADVANCE OF A DRUG RAID in the summer of 1995, my team gathered for a briefing at a patrol station. When the undercover officer who was to conduct the briefing walked across the parking lot toward the entrance door, I could not help but stare. She was petite and brown-skinned with long wavy hair. She had a broad smile and a gorgeous figure. The moment she began speaking, her accent and attitude revealed where she was from—New York City. She was at once confident and classy, using hand gestures to emphasize her most important points. It is no surprise that I, the son of a powerful woman, found this woman's strength and presence attractive. She introduced herself as Cedonia.

After the briefing, I pulled her sergeant aside. He and I were friends. "Is she married?" I asked.

"No," he said.

"Do you know if she's dating anyone?"

He shook his head. Then as I walked off, he said, "Brown, don't mess with her." Cops have a "love 'em and leave 'em" reputation, and as Cedonia's supervisor, he felt protective of her. "I won't," I reassured him. "I seriously like her." And I meant it.

A few weeks later when I ran into Cedonia, I approached her. "May I take you to lunch?" I asked, conjuring up the most gentleman-sounding voice I could. Long gone were the years when I felt shy about even talking to a girl. By this time, I was in the best shape of my life, with a coveted spot on a premier squad, and I won't lie: I didn't lack confidence. Cedonia smiled at me. "Sure," she said without hesitation. "I'd love to."

We hit it off on date one. Cedonia was chatty, funny, spirited—and an excellent storyteller. She did most of the talking (like any self-respecting New Yorker), and I hung on her every word. I could tell she was both intelligent and sincere. She was also ambitious: She was a few years younger than me yet had already earned an MBA. That first date turned into a second, a fifth, and a tenth. I don't think she fell for me as quickly as I did for her, but after a couple months of seeing each other exclusively, we were both all in.

From day one, we kept our relationship off the radar. Because our divisions often collaborated, I was concerned that, if the news got out, one of us might be transferred. I trusted my friend, Cedonia's supervisor, to stay quiet. And for me, keeping a low profile was second nature. Both Cedonia and I, who'd spent our careers in the public eye, have always been fairly private when it comes to our personal lives. As far as we were concerned, our relationship was our business.

Dating Cedonia felt so right to me, so easy and comfortable from the very beginning. We understood the intensity of each other's jobs. She knew the details of the raids I'd been involved in, especially since we both worked graveyard. She also knew how to let me be silent after a particularly grueling shift. My retreat didn't threaten her. She knew where it came from and didn't take it personally. Having both confronted perilous situations for a living, we recognized each other's need to disconnect. For me, it was relationship bliss.

AFTER THE ARIZONA AVENUE SHOOTING, I was determined to never again let my team get caught flat-footed by gunfire when approaching a drug house. We often used flash bangs, the kind we'd thrown in on that machete-wielding man. If, after we'd thrown a flash bang into the window, the suspects came out shooting, we'd at least be in a strong position to take cover and possibly eliminate the need for gunfire. In my mind, that is always priority number one: Minimize the use of force in order to maximize safety.

That was my squad's plan when we showed up at an apartment building in East Dallas. The entire complex, controlled by a group of big-time dope dealers, was drug infested. Another New Jack City. Residents in the area had been complaining nonstop for months, understandably; living in the vicinity of a drug house, they were walking around in fear of random gunfire. So our narcotics detectives secured a warrant, and we prepared to shut down the place, starting with the ground-floor apartment the dealers shared.

My team threw in a flash bang, and seconds later the drapes on the front windows burst into flames. The dealers came running out, coughing and holding their hands up in full surrender. As officers made the arrests, I and a new member of the squad, Joe Maines, whom we affectionately called "Broadway Joe" because he's debonair and always dressed sharply, prepared to go in and put out the fire; we also needed to ensure no one else was still inside. We donned our smoke masks and made our way through the front door. In the living room, we tried to stomp out the flames that had engulfed the drapes. That didn't work. As the fire burned, I ran toward the interior rooms to complete the search. No one else was in the apartment. While I was in the back bedroom, I heard the detective shout out something, but I couldn't understand him. When I returned to the living room, I realized what he'd been trying to tell me—get out. Just in that short time, the fire had spread to every part of the living room, its hot flames spitting out in every direction. The doorway we'd entered through was completely enveloped in flames. Joe had refused to leave without me.

We searched for a window, but amid the plumes of smoke, we couldn't find one. As we crawled around on the floor, my breathing became labored. Even with the masks on, it was impossible not to inhale some smoke. Joe finally spotted a window, stood, and used a nearby chair to break the glass. "Sarge, come over here!" he shouted. We both lunged through the window and rolled out onto a grassy area right beneath it.

I looked up to see the last face I expected—Cedonia's. "Are you all right?" she asked as I coughed, trying to catch my breath. When she'd heard about the fire on the police radio, she'd asked her supervisor whether I'd been hurt. "I don't know," he told her, "but I know the apartment is on fire." She then raced to the scene. When she arrived, the other cops on my squad must've suspected there was something going on between us, but we still tried to act as if there weren't.

The EMTs took me to the hospital, where I remained overnight for observation. I was put on oxygen to clear the smoke in my lungs. I was also treated for the minor injury I'd sustained when breaking out of that window; I'd been cut by the broken glass. Cedonia urged me to receive a tetanus shot, but I don't like needles—especially when it involves a long needle right into your behind. She eventually won that battle, and I endured the shot.

After Joe and I escaped from the building, the complex was eventually lost to the flames—the fire department could not salvage a single unit. I expected there to be endless paperwork in the aftermath, particularly since my decision to throw in a flash bang had ignited the fire. Surely a lawsuit would be filed. But in the following weeks, there was not a single ounce of pushback. Not from those who'd been evacuated from the building during the fire and subsequently lost their homes. Not from the property owner. And of course, not from the area residents who'd been complaining about the drug house. I'm sure they were happy to see the place go.

A towering inferno. A dedicated girlfriend. Machetes and crawl spaces. A joyous son. All in a year and a half's work on SWAT.

CHAPTER 10

TRANSITIONS

—

W ORD GOT OUT THAT CEDONIA AND I WERE DATING. AS big as Dallas is, it can feel like a small village, as it did when one of Cedonia's fellow narcotics detectives spotted us at a Frankie Beverly and Maze concert in 1995. Cedonia and I entered the stadium holding hands. After we ran into her colleagues, I told her, "This ain't gonna be a secret much longer." I was right. By the next day, everyone on SWAT knew we were a couple and teased me. Thankfully, neither of us was asked to transfer to another department.

As our romance blossomed, I began exploring our compatibilities beyond basic attraction. In particular, I wanted to be sure we were on the same page financially. In the early 1980s, I'd taken out a mortgage on a small home in an affordable Dallas suburb. I felt a great sense of accomplishment in at last reaching that milestone. But amid my divorce, I'd had to sell it. In the following years, I'd slowly rebuilt my savings with the intent of buying my next house outright. I'm an extreme saver, a cheap bastard, some would say: I've never spent much on extravagant jewelry, cars, clothes, or vacations. I wait for holiday sales to buy a couple of quality suits. I've owned two cars in my whole adult life. And every time I was promoted and received a pay raise, I socked away the extra in my 401(k) and continued living on my patrol cop salary. I lived way below my means.

At thirty-two, I reached my goal of becoming debt-free. I also purchased a plot of land and paid cash for a house in North Dallas. I had that home relocated from its lot onto my land. With only taxes and insurance to pay, and no car note, I could save virtually all the earnings from my moonlighting work. My plan was to work for twenty years and then retire in peace and plenty, while still young enough to pursue an entrepreneurial interest. I was striving for financial independence, as well as wealth to pass on to the next generation, something no one in my family had ever accomplished. That felt like a worthwhile goal, a reason to keep working as many hours as I could. By the time Cedonia and I started dating seriously, I had enough sense to realize that I should consider whether she shared my views on financial matters. She did. Though she's not as conservative as I am, she's definitely a saver.

I introduced Cedonia to my parents. They adored her. She and I spent most of our time away from work together. The trust between us built with each caring gesture. We fell deeply in love. If I was sick, she wouldn't leave my side; the same was true for me. Our relationship was based not on material things but on an authentic friendship and soulmate connection. We enjoyed the kind of companionship and love that seems scarce in today's world. As with all things rare, I cherished it as priceless.

I TOOK CEDONIA ON a short trip to San Antonio in the spring of 1996. "It'll be fun to get away for a weekend, just the two of us," I told her. She excitedly agreed. Unbeknownst to her, I also had something else in mind: I was planning to propose. Months before, we'd talked about marriage, and I'd even taken her with me to pick out a ring. One of my SWAT buddies was best friends with a jeweler who cut diamonds himself. He'd agreed to give me a wholesale price on a ring I wouldn't have otherwise been able to afford. We ordered it, and I awaited its arrival. But I hadn't yet shown it to Cedonia or even told her that it had come in.

For the first evening of our getaway, I'd made a reservation at a restaurant called the Landing, which faced the River Walk. Before dinner, we strolled hand in hand along the boardwalk, the glistening waters reflecting the moon's soft glow. Once we were seated inside and enjoying our meal, the members of a jazz band began setting up onstage for the evening's entertainment. That's when I had an idea.

I excused myself to the men's room and pulled aside our waitress. "I'm about to propose to my girlfriend," I whispered to her. "Is there any way I can do it up on the stage in front of everyone?" With a wink and a nod, she was in. She told the bandleader of my plan as I waited out of Cedonia's sight.

The bandleader introduced the musicians. "And tonight," he ended by saying, "we have a special performer. His name is

David Brown, and he's here all the way from Dallas. Give him a round of applause!" The restaurant's patrons clapped loudly. I strode up onto the stage. As I took the mic, you should have seen the look on Cedonia's face! She mouthed, *What are you doing?*

I just grinned. "Cedonia Butts," I said, "please come to the stage."

With surprise written all over her expression, she made her way to the front. I then pulled out the diamond ring from my suit pocket and dropped down onto my knee. "Will you marry me?" I asked her. She cupped her hands over her face and began to bawl. "Yes," she said through tears. As we embraced and I slid the ring onto her finger, the room erupted in applause. Later, our angel-of-a-waitress popped us a bottle of champagne on the house.

We did not want a protracted engagement period or an elaborate wedding in a huge church. We're both low maintenance. So we chose Jordan Missionary Baptist Church just outside Dallas. After the pastor there guided us through premarital counseling, we eventually traded vows with our family members and friends gathered around.

I'D ALWAYS MADE IT a priority to spend time with D.J., but the demands and sacrifices of serving on the force took me away from home and my son more often than I wanted. Soon after my son was born, I entered the police academy and began work as a patrol cop. By D.J.'s fifth birthday in 1988, I'd become a crime scene investigator. And for most of my son's teen years, I served in SWAT, a job as emotionally grueling as it is physically demanding.

And yet even while soldiering through eighteen-hour days, I found as much time as I could to spend with D.J. I'd often stop by, unannounced and still in my uniform, to visit him in his elementary school classroom. Once he entered junior high and started playing in the band, I never missed a concert. Seated in the stands, I'd look on with pride as the notes rang out from his trombone. My son, like my brother Rickey, had shown musical talent from a young age. With no training, D.J. could deliver the most perfect, soulful rendition of any song he heard. Though he had the natural gift of playing by ear, he also learned to read music. He put his all into every note.

Following the divorce in 1988, D.J. lived with his mother and stepsister; he visited me every other weekend. That changed in the summer of 1996, the year he turned thirteen—and the year Cedonia and I married. Like many teenagers, D.J. began challenging his mother's authority. His grades had slipped. I instinctively knew what my son was missing: more time with his father. A few weeks before the start of his eighth-grade year, his mother and I agreed that he would come and live with me.

Even before D.J. moved in, he knew I'd be strict. I did not underdeliver on that expectation. In our home, Cedonia, who immediately embraced D.J. as if he were her own son, served as the primary consoler. I, though a compassionate father, became the disciplinarian. Weekly chores were to be completed. Instructions were to be followed with no back talk. All homework was to be done thoroughly and handed in on time. In his elementary school years, my son had earned the highest marks with minimal effort. He'd always been smart. I knew what he was capable of if he applied himself.

And he did. During that fall semester, D.J.'s grades improved dramatically, as did his attitude. We had a few bristles when he first arrived—most adolescents push the boundaries as they stretch toward independence. But once D.J. realized my standards were nonnegotiable, he settled down and returned to being the child I'd known him as: affable and easygoing, warm and socially engaged, kind and respectful. That behavior continued through the remainder of junior high and throughout high school.

YOU KNOW BY NOW that I have a healthy dose of ambition. That drive, coupled with my daily awareness of the plans Walter and I had once laid out for ourselves, motivated me to continue moving up in the department. As 1997 drew to a close, I'd already been in SWAT for four years and had settled happily into married life. I felt ready for the next challenge. So when the opportunity arose for me to take the exam to become a lieutenant, I jumped at it. Dozens of officers applied for only a handful of open slots, and the test was more difficult than any previous ones I'd taken. To have a chance, I knew my score would have to be high enough to make me one of the top ten candidates. I also knew I'd have to ace the interview. The challenge didn't scare me away; in fact, it fueled my competitiveness.

More than a year before the test, I began studying. I felt like I was back in college: flash cards, practice tests, constant reading. Speaking of undergrad, I also re-enrolled around that time. It had always bothered me that I'd never finished my degree, and I figured that while I was already in a study groove, it was a good time to pick up some classes. I transferred my earlier credits to Dallas Baptist University in Oak Cliff, which was conveniently located on my way to work. Initially, I tried to balance all this with my SWAT job and moonlighting gig as a security officer at a bank. That didn't last. I eventually dropped the side job and focused solely on my studies.

In 1998, I passed the written lieutenant's exam but didn't do well enough on the interview to land the job. Eight officers had been chosen, and my score on the interview was ninth. The disappointment fueled me to try again, and in 1999, I reapplied. When my interview score turned out to be the fourth highest, I was promoted to lieutenant. Later that year, after taking one class at a time during every fall, winter, spring, and summer term over the course of a year, I crossed another goal off my list. I earned a bachelor's degree in business, and a year and a half later I completed an MBA as well. Coach Hulcy, my fifth-grade football coach, was proven right yet again: What at first looks like failure can become sweet triumph the second time around.

COLUMBINE CHANGED POLICING IN AMERICA. The high school massacre occurred on April 20, 1999, the year I became a lieutenant. As the gruesome details unfolded, the nation was at once devastated and transfixed by the horrifying news: In Littleton, Colorado, teenage schoolboys Eric Harris and Dylan Klebold had murdered twelve of their classmates and a teacher and wounded twenty-four others before killing themselves. It was a turning point in our nation's collective consciousness as well as a wake-up call for police.

Columbine, of course, was far from the first mass shooting within our borders. In 1966, a notorious killing occurred at the University of Texas at Austin, when gunman Charles Whitman opened fire from the college's tower building. By the end of his spree, Whitman had murdered fourteen people and injured thirty-one. Such massacres have occurred at various points in human history, but until the 1960s and beyond, most were felony-related or involved the killing of family members. Since the Whitman murders, there had been a steady uptick in a particular brand of violence: random gunfire against innocent bystanders in public places.

It was the norm in the 1990s for patrol officers to serve as first responders to a shooting spree, which at that point typically involved a pistol or handgun. Meanwhile SWAT would be on its way to negotiate with the gunman and lead him to surrender or, if that didn't work, take him down. That tactic shifted after Columbine. We all witnessed shooters intent on meting out terror, usually wielding multiple assault weapons with high-capacity bullet storage, giving them the ability to take the lives of dozens before SWAT could even arrive. In police departments around the country, including in Dallas, cops at every level began receiving training in how to manage and stop an active shooter. In addition, SWAT teams kept their vans equipped with weaponry powerful enough to rival the automatic machine guns and explosives used by these assailants.

Once upon a time, it was rare for an officer—and particularly a beat cop—to ever be shot at or to shoot his or her weapon. I spent nearly a decade on the force before I had to fire my gun for the first time, during the Arizona Avenue showdown. But with the advent of the active shooter, the use of deadly force—as well as the militarization of policing overall—has become increasingly common and, in my view, necessary. I can only hope that the trend will reverse. Yet in light of the never-ending headlines involving senseless carnage at the hands of those who seek to destroy, I'm not sure it will.

Few of us could have predicted the torrent of mass shootings that would follow Columbine. In 2007, Virginia Tech student Seung-Hui Cho mowed down thirty-two innocent people on that university's campus in southwestern Virginia. In 2012, in the deadliest grade-school shooting in U.S. history, Adam Lanza murdered twenty kindergarteners and first graders and six staff members at Sandy Hook Elementary School in Newtown, Connecticut. In June 2015, Dylann Roof, a self-proclaimed white supremacist, attended a prayer meeting at a church in Charleston, South Carolina, and then opened fire, killing nine black worshipers. Months later Rizwan Farook and Tashfeen Malik, a married couple, gunned down fourteen people at a holiday party in San Bernardino, California. The Orlando nightclub shooting, carried out by Omar Mateen, left fifty people dead and another fifty-three wounded. The list goes on.

In so many of these cases, the assailants have been mentally ill. And yet as the casualty counts climb, our country's laws allow even the most emotionally disturbed individuals to freely access potent firearms—which can be anonymously purchased, in a few clicks, on the Internet.

MY OLD MAN CAME to my lieutenant promotion ceremony. Though he was in and out of my life, he'd occasionally appear on the scene—and this was one of those times. After the ceremony, he and my commanders, including Chief Ben Click, who'd been leading the department since 1993, got into a long conversation. I tried to hear what they were talking about but couldn't. After they'd talked for a full fifteen minutes, they shook hands and dispersed.

My father then pulled me aside. "Son," he said, looking directly into my eyes, "I want you to know that I'm proud of you."

I stared at him for a long moment, unsure of what to say in return and wondering what had prompted his statement.

"Thank you," I said, hugging him. "I appreciate that, Dad."

Later that evening my father told me what he and my commanders had been discussing: my work over sixteen years in the department. I seldom shared any details about my policing adventures, and particularly my SWAT operations, with anyone in my family. If my mom truly understood the risk my job carried, it would've frightened her to death. My father, the one voice of dissent when I joined the force, at last understood my work through a different lens—from the viewpoint of those who'd worked alongside me, witnessed my professional growth, and promoted me. "They have big plans for you," my father told me. "They really respect you."

Before that day, I hadn't consciously yearned for my father's affirmation. It was only after he'd uttered a sentence I'd never heard him say—"I'm proud of you, son"—that I realized how I'd always craved his approval, his acknowledgment of my work, man to man. His words resonated powerfully. His recognition meant the world to me.

I was thirty-nine at the time. I'd long before made peace with the man my father had been when I was growing up. He'd made mistakes, many he lived to regret. Maya Angelou once said, "I did then what I knew how to do. Now that I know better, I do better." The same was as true for my father as it is for each of us. Be it during childhood or years after, we come to see our parents as they are, especially as we view ourselves more clearly: at times heroic, yes, but ultimately flawed and human.

I didn't know it at the time, but my conversation with my father that day would be the last meaningful one we'd ever share. That year, after a long battle with lung disease, my dad passed away at the age of fifty-nine. His spirit transitioned, but his words, spoken with love and tenderness, have lived on.

BACK WHEN I'D FIRST joined the force in 1983, Billy Prince had been our chief. During his six-year tenure, he began what he called neighborhood policing, opening storefront police offices in communities around Dallas. The stations, usually in strip malls, were staffed by cops. Members of the surrounding community could walk in and directly interact with an officer—to offer a complaint, give a tip, or just talk—at any time of the day or night. The program did not go over well among officers. The patrol cops assigned to these storefronts had been accustomed to fielding high-stakes, adrenaline-inducing emergencies. "Who's going to handle the 911 calls while these officers are sitting around at a storefront?" complained many who didn't see the new approach as real police work. Unions also protested.

Enter Ben Click, who took over the DPD five years after Prince moved on. In response to police shootings and the political pressure to be more responsive to residents' needs, Click created a new and improved neighborhood policing program called Interactive Community Policing (ICP), a 2.0 version in which officers were no longer relegated entirely to storefronts; instead, units of four or five cops at every police substation were assigned to specialize in community policing, which they could do while riding around the city on patrol. Even so some of the storefronts still existed, and under Click, other storefront-style stations were added—many of which were in or near housing developments.

Those chosen as ICP cops were to regularly meet with citizens' groups such as homeowners' associations and PTAs, both to brief them on area crime and to hear and address their concerns. These officers were also responsible for building neighborhood watch groups from the ground up, often by going door-to-door. The whole point of the program was to build community relationships that led to trust and, ultimately, to a safer city. That was Click's vision. While his expanded program was more popular than the one Prince had rolled out, it was still met with resistance, from the old-school officers in particular. I was one of those officers.

When I became lieutenant, Chief Click gave me my first assignment—as supervisor of an ICP station in a West Dallas housing development, then one of the city's largest and most violent. In other words, Click was sending me to a six-hundred-square-foot apartment that had been converted into a police substation right in the middle of the projects. Before I could launch a campaign in protest, Doug Kowalski—the supervisor who, in the break room, had once offered me a way out of the 911 Center—made his own appeal to the department's top brass. "I need Brown to stay on in SWAT as lieutenant," he told

Click. But for reasons he did not reveal to Doug or me, the chief was resolute.

I was downright agitated. During my sixteen years on the job, I'd been chasing burglars and murderers. Shutting down crack houses. Hurling flash bangs. And defusing the tensest hostage and kidnapping situations imaginable. I'd even been on the SWAT team that had survived one of Dallas's most horrendous gun battles. And now I was supposed to trade all that in to sip tea with grandmothers and hobnob with the locals? Just the thought of it made me yawn. The television heroes I'd admired so much as a child would've never been sitting around, picking their noses, while others fought the real battles to vanquish crime. Perry Mason wouldn't have done it; nor would Batman or Superman. And if Walter had still been alive, I was sure he'd refuse. Community policing, in theory and on paper, sounded like a fine idea—as long as someone other than me had to take it on.

OPERATION KITCHEN SINK

———

S OME COPS ARE NATURALS AT COMMUNITY POLICING. Without even thinking about it, they chat up residents in their patrol areas and gather information on the neighborhood's greatest needs. They don't have to be told to take an approach that's more proactive than reactive, one in which building trust with citizens is at the front end of the crime-solving equation. Chief Click had, I'm sure, recognized those in the department who had that inclination and assigned them to ICP. Which makes it all the more puzzling why he chose me—a cop who gloried in locking away villains. A lieutenant who preferred drug raids to social mixers. If my old man had been right that Click had big things in mind for me, this was a strange way for him to show it.

Every day began with a foot patrol. I supervised a team of twelve officers, and we'd take turns walking through the complex, around the courtyard, upstairs and downstairs along the corridors. This was one of Dallas's largest housing develop-ments, so there were hundreds of residents, and I didn't wait for an invitation to talk to any of them. Since I had to be there, I figured I might as well make things interesting. "How are you-all doing?" I'd ask, wandering up to pairs of older women who sat out on their terraces. "What's going on?" They'd smile and nod and welcome me with sweet Southern accents. A few resi-dents initially seemed reluctant to talk to me, but the vast majority embraced me. There was an instant familiarity and kinship: When I connected with the people there, I felt like I was talking to my great-grandmother, Mabel. Or my mother, Norma Jean. Or the classmates I'd played sports with. The con-versations were as easy and comfortable as they were relaxed and friendly.

Beyond strolling, I did a whole lot of hanging out. I was on hand for barbecues and block parties. I shot hoops with the kids down at a nearby recreation center. My team and I organized a crime watch task force and met with parents from the local PTA. And never once did I answer a 911 call. Like the rest of my team, I was there to gather intel and pass it along to Dis-patch so they could send in other officers to handle the emer-gencies. And on occasion, I did get a tip.

After I'd been on the job for a few months, people began confiding in me, giving me criminal intelligence that officers could act on to improve safety. I noticed that the officers who'd been assigned there had keen insight into people's lives, knew their kids and other relatives, and could distinguish the criminal element from the good folks whose only crime was being poor, locked in generational poverty. I recall one instance in which a shooting that had happened on the previous night became the talk of the neighborhood the next day. Soon the officers on my team knew the name of the shooter, where he lived, the car he drove, and his baby mama's name and address. This information came in so quickly because the officers were trusted in the community and people believed that something would be done to capture the shooter if they came forward. They knew our cops wouldn't give them up as snitches. This incident was a wake-up call for me: Community policing could lead to solving crimes, even violent ones.

Such criminal intelligence and subsequent action was off-putting to lawbreakers. The constant presence of officers sent a message, loud and clear, to thieves and dope dealers: *This is no longer your turf. Your community is reclaiming it.* Crooks tend to feed off anonymity and fear. They count on their neighbors being scared to call 911 and report them. Even those in my complex who would report a robbery wouldn't, for instance, reveal that it was their own home that was being robbed. They didn't want word to get back to the robber, often someone right there in the housing complex. The most powerful way officers can begin reversing that dynamic is to shift the perception of who owns the building. And the corner. You want the citizens there to realize *they* own it. And when the people take back this ownership, the criminals become paranoid.

Let's say our police department hosts a block party. Residents are milling around outdoors, enjoying free popcorn and hot dogs. And throughout the afternoon, most of them are stopping by to talk with the cops who are there. There's little fear of being spotted and singled out for chatting with cops, because dozens of people are doing the same. Believe me, the criminals in the crowd are taking in the whole scene. But they

Mom and Dad cutting the cake on their wedding day in 1958.

My father, Walter Lee Brown—charismatic and confident—
in our Oak Cliff home.

Norma Jean
Brown—
my beautiful,
classy mother—
holding me
steady and
wearing her
signature smile.

Mabel Henderson, my maternal great-grandmother and
our family's matriarch—a nurturing presence in my life.

My pre-K class photo for the small Catholic school my older brother Ricky and I attended.

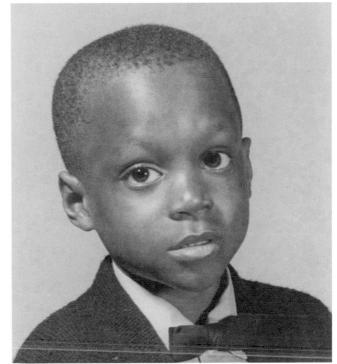

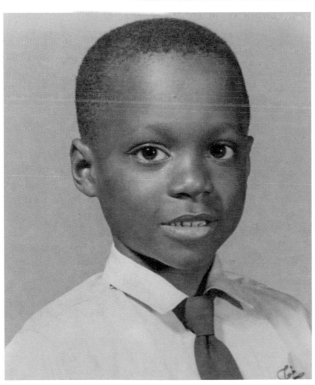

In first grade at Roger Q. Mills Elementary School, where my teachers would instill in me the confidence and expectation that I could succeed academically.

My brothers and me
(from left: me,
Kelvin, and Ricky).

Dressed in our
finest threads
(from left: me,
Kelvin, and Ricky).

My mother's big boys
(from left: me, Kelvin,
and Ricky).

Singing my heart out as a soloist in fourth grade.

A Texas kid in San Francisco, 1975.

Mark Twain Elementary School class photo in 1973. Mike Shillinburg is in the middle of the second row wearing a red sweater. I'm just behind him, top row, center.

Posing for my family in cap
and gown before heading to my
high school graduation.

Most Likely To Succeed

David Brown

"Most Likely to Succeed,"
South Oak Cliff High School,
Class of 1979.
(I was also voted
"Most Intellectual" that year.)

Embracing the dawn of a
new existence, on my own
two feet—freshman year
at UT Austin.

Becoming an officer meant answering the most important call of my life.

The forty-first
president of the
United States,
George H. W. Bush,
expresses his thanks for
dignitary protection.

Best Wishes to
Sergeant David Brown

G Bush

My son, D. J., meets the
forty-second president
of the United States,
Bill Clinton.

Vice-President
Al Gore offers
thanks for dignitary
protection.

To Sergeant David Brown
With best wishes,

Al Gore

In action, responding to riots in the city after the Dallas Cowboys won the 1993 Super Bowl.

As SWAT sergeant, with my squad, following the Arizona Avenue raid—grateful to be alive.

Embracing my wife, Cedonia, on our wedding day, 1996.

Having a partner in life who understood the
intensity of the job was relationship bliss.

My older brother, Ricky, by my side after I'd received my new lieutenant badge.

The Dallas branch of the NAACP celebrated my appointment as one of the nation's few black police chiefs—Dallas's second.

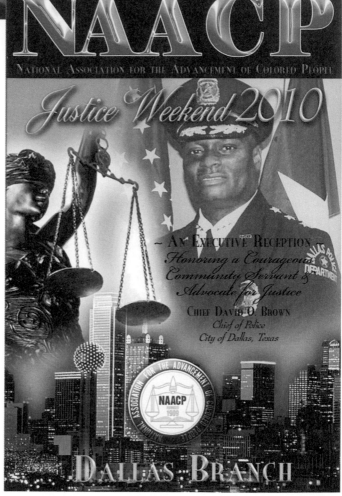

NAACP
NATIONAL ASSOCIATION FOR THE ADVANCEMENT OF COLORED PEOPLE

Justice Weekend 2010

~ An Executive Reception
Honoring a Courageous
Community Servant &
Advocate for Justice

CHIEF DAVID O. BROWN
Chief of Police
City of Dallas, Texas

NAACP
FOUNDED
1909

DALLAS BRANCH

Fatigue, anguish, and heartbreak—standing at the funerals
of our fallen comrades, July 2016.

My private grief, not my decades of public service, had best prepared me for this moment.

Cedonia and me with the forty-third president of the United States, George W. Bush, and former first lady Laura Bush.

To David Brown
With best wishes,

Proudly shaking hands with the forty-fourth president
of the United States, Barack Obama.

have no idea whether one of their neighbors' interactions with an officer is an innocuous hello or a tattle session. They're thinking, *Could that person be snitching on me?* Maybe all the guy is saying is "Man, that Cowboys game on Sunday was crazy"—but from afar, the criminal can't hear that conversation.

That's when paranoia sets in. With all these people potentially running their mouths to cops, it suddenly seems riskier to burglarize a home in that area. A place where, previously, they had broken the law with impunity has now become one in which they have to constantly look over their shoulder. And a little at a time, what once felt like their stomping ground becomes an uncomfortable environment in which to commit a crime.

Oddly, officers can identify with the criminal's state of mind. They often share a similar psychological profile. Hypervigilance is paranoia by another name. That's what makes many officers uniquely qualified to use psychological warfare in dealing with offenders. We understand how they view the world and can use that to our advantage. If I'm interviewing a murder suspect, I'm going to bluff that I have far more evidence than I do, just to make him panic and confess. Or in an alternative approach, I'm going to say "You thirsty, man? Here, have a Coke"—and just as he's reaching for it, you make him first write down his account. Or if I'm trying to get a hostile barricaded person to come out of his house, I'm going to pretend I'll use force, the way I once did with those robbers hiding in the crawl space. The games we cops play are fun as hell, and especially when I was in SWAT, I got hooked on them.

But I digress. The whole time I was in that apartment complex, as much as I had started to see the value in a different approach, I was itching to get back into the action. I was craving the addictive high of my previous job, and leaving it behind had triggered a slow and painful withdrawal. Nearly every day I still had lunch with my buddies on my former SWAT squad. When I wasn't with them, I was calling to check in: "What are you-all doing today?" I'd ask. "Any new raids?" In retrospect, it was sad and pathetic, not to mention funny. I was so eager to get out of there that, within a couple months of taking on the job, I started looking for an exit strategy.

It didn't help that, while I got along well with the residents, I wasn't a fan of some of the officers on my team. Our personalities didn't mesh. And aside from that, I'd come in with an attitude, a judgment that the "soft policing" they were doing behind the scenes gave them zero street cred. But I was wrong. Dead wrong.

I FINALLY LEFT THE PROJECTS after a year and a half and skipped around town to various patrol stations. In 2001, I was transferred to South Dallas, then a tough part of the city. Different location and colleagues, same mandate to supervise a team implementing a robust community policing program. I was then transferred to the Northeast patrol division as a lieutenant for a year, and three years later, I was promoted to deputy chief of that division—making me one of about fifteen officers at that rank.

It was during those two ICP assignments that I first noticed my instincts had slowly shifted: I couldn't do traditional policing without automatically thinking about how to incorporate community policing. I found myself looking for ways to get every cop on my team, even those who were answering 911 calls, to connect with the people they served. And I encouraged my officers to set up neighborhood watch groups. That first assignment in the housing development had clearly planted a seed.

I also started realizing some hard truths about the work I'd done earlier in my career. In the 1980s and '90s, I'd been part of the major push to lock up hundreds of offenders, starting with the Reagan-era expansion of the War on Drugs and the "Just Say No" campaign, and continuing with the 1994 crime bill during President Bill Clinton's first term. Zero tolerance was the order of the day as public concern and outcry about drug use reached a point of hysteria. Along with it came draconian three-strikes policies that hit poor communities the hardest and disproportionately impacted black men. During that period, America became the country with the highest incarceration rate in the world.

Dallas was especially hard hit. The reality is that during the 1990s, Dallas experienced the highest crime rate in its history, and that high rate continued through 2004 and beyond, as we locked away more and more people. It would seem, at first glance, that throwing these offenders in jail would be the best approach. And yet my experience after decades on the ground told a different story. While keeping prisons full has lined the pockets of those who run the prison industry, it hasn't necessarily made us safer—particularly inner-city residents. As a beat cop, I'd send someone to jail, only to see that person right back on the street a week or a month later, committing the same crime. Prison was a revolving door. While murderers and bank robbers usually received long sentences, drug offenders were often released within days, soon after they'd been probated and paroled. They'd then get out and look for work, and when no one would hire them because of their criminal records, they'd rob to get money. Instead of rehabilitating them, our system had set them up to become career criminals. Over time, these realizations got me thinking: *If locking people up is so effective, then why do I keep throwing the exact same people in jail? And what is the alternative?*

THERE'S NO PERFECT ANSWER or cure-all. Mass incarceration did not happen in a vacuum; its beginnings coincided with a public school system that was beginning to deteriorate at the moment we started putting more people in prison. It also coincided with the defunding of mental health and drug treatment programs for the one-third of prisoners who are mentally ill. These factors, among others, converged to form a perfect storm that ultimately left certain neighborhoods broken and in disarray.

During my back-to-back community policing assignments, I hadn't been there to put anyone in jail. In place of hauling off dealers to prison, I was building relationships with young kids, trying to put them on the right path years before they could be sucked into a life of crime. I was just talking to people—or at least that's what it seemed like on the surface. And yet one interaction at a time, many of those residents began to see us as part of their community's extended family. On a daily basis, I was reminded of all the reasons I got into policing in the first place—to serve others and to change lives. I'd been doing that, of course, by tracking down criminals. But this brand of policing was less about a foot chase and more about face time. It required me to put aside my need for the adrenaline rush of locking away criminals, which, in retrospect, seems driven more by self-aggrandizement than by a desire to serve. The whole point of community policing is to create safer communities, and it had slowly dawned on me that that doesn't have to involve a gun. In fact, the greatest weapon in an officer's arsenal can be a passing conversation with a resident on the block. That brief connection can be a significant source of power.

CHIEF DAVID KUNKLE STEPPED into the top job in 2004. Years earlier he'd joined DPD as a rookie before eventually moving on to the police department in Arlington, a suburb just outside the city. There he'd worked his way up the ranks to become deputy city manager. He traded that job to take on the most significant in his career: slashing crime in Dallas, which then, as I've said, had the highest violent crime rate among the nation's big cities. He'd started by implementing a CompStat model of policing—a statistical metric system, introduced in 1994 by Commissioner Bill Bratton of the New York City Police Department. It was used to track crime, combat petty offenses as a way to reduce bigger ones, and foster officer accountability. I call it the show-me approach to law enforcement: Don't just tell me how good you are at your job—demonstrate it by revealing how many fewer robberies you had last week.

Not long after Chief Kunkle took the helm, he called a CompStat meeting with the department's commanders. After laying out his vision for expanding our community policing efforts, he concluded by giving us a challenge.

"Bring me one win," he told the group. "I need one small win from every one of you. Just one." He didn't define what a "win" would look like; nor did he give an example. He simply left it open for our interpretation. When I heard the chief's request, I took it seriously. Right then and there in that conference room, I quietly resolved that I would somehow create a small miracle. After leaving the housing development, I'd been assigned to Lake Highlands, a community in the northeast patrol division of Dallas. I would make it my personal mission to deliver a win there.

Historically, Lake Highlands hadn't been a particularly crime-ridden suburb. In fact, I'd always known it to be affluent. As a kid when I passed through the mostly white area on a bus ride, the people I spotted on the front lawns of luxurious homes always felt a world away from my own neighborhood—and their world was one I dreamed of inhabiting. But the scene there changed when, in the late 1990s, a cluster of apartment complexes that had been built a decade earlier were opened to low-income residents. As they moved in, that pocket of the neighborhood became an eyesore and an aggravation for those whose nice homes butted up against the dilapidated buildings. The crime rate inched up. Burglaries and drug deals became commonplace. And longtime residents had no shortage of complaints.

For days after Chief Kunkle's challenge, I drove around thinking about what my win could be. I talked to community members and called up city council members. I knew most wanted to generally cut crime in that disruptive area, but I wanted to get more specific. "What is the one place where we most need to make a change?" I asked. A consensus emerged:

The street corner at the intersection of Forest Lane and Audelia Road was the epicenter, the place from which much of the neighborhood's crime emanated. "If you can get us a win there," council members Bill Blaydes and Gary Griffith told me, "we'll be one hundred percent behind you from now on."

Many residents said the same. Up until then, officers had tried just about every strategy to clean up that intersection, even bringing in narcotics officers to host community gatherings. And yet that corner was still giving everyone the blues. "Nothing has worked," one sergeant admitted. "We've thrown everything but the kitchen sink at the problem." His comment gave me an idea: Why not at last throw the kitchen sink at the situation? That's how Operation Kitchen Sink came to life. It would be my plan for scoring a win.

Many communities have a corner exactly like the one at Forest and Audelia. The criminals are there, operating in broad daylight, because they feel they can. Who is going to stop them? No one. And in Lake Highlands, they'd gotten particularly bold: Even when patrol cops rode by, they'd keep right on doing what they were doing. Officers had been working hard to combat crime in the area, but their efforts weren't moving the needle—and the problem had become so overwhelming that they didn't know how to proceed. What had been true during my assignment in the housing development was also true here: When criminals feel comfortable, they wreak havoc. They act like they own the place, and if no one stops them, they will expand their territory. That's what happened in *New Jack City,* when Nino Brown took over an entire apartment building and ran his crack operation from there. I wasn't having it. That's why my kitchen sink strategy began with 24/7 supervision of that corner. With the help of the officers in my substation, I was determined to take back that intersection by, for starters, never leaving it.

And that is what my team and I did. At the start of my shift, I'd stop in at the convenience store there and buy myself a bottle of Big Red soda or an RC and a large bag of Lay's potato chips, my favorite. I'd then return to my nearby squad car and wait. And watch. And wait some more. The same way I used to wait for drug users to back out too fast from a driveway. The absence of activity became our first triumph. Within days after we began our around-the-clock coverage, crime plummeted. The 911 calls dissipated. The dealers traded their dope elsewhere. After just two weeks of constant surveillance, that intersection went from a bustling superhighway of criminal activity to one of the safest and quietest corners in the city. A second win soon followed: The crime dip spread from that corner to other parts of the area. Our efforts had a ripple effect. The results were specific, measurable, and undeniable.

With our triumph came a lesson that became the premise of my policing strategy: To reduce crime, you needn't target an entire substation or even a hundred blocks. Rather, you have to focus on transforming the hot spot—the one place, like that intersection, that has become ground zero for criminal activity in the area. By transforming it, you will automatically put criminals on edge. And in that window immediately after they scatter or go underground, officers have an opportunity to engage and empower community members. The citizens of Lake Highlands were too frightened to do anything about that corner until it was clear. But once it had been reclaimed, my team organized residents and equipped them with the tools they needed to keep it that way—by, for example, alerting neighborhood officers of any suspicious activity or calling 911. I was so hell-bent on keeping that corner clear that I offered residents my personal cellphone number. "If we don't do what we've promised to do at this intersection," I told them at a community gathering, "I want you to call me directly, any time of the day or night"—and boy, did they call. The progress we made was sustainable only because we'd gotten the community involved and invested.

The residents' response to our small win was off the charts. Chief Kunkle also took notice. Operation Kitchen Sink was the most successful tactic I'd ever implemented, and for me, it became a pivot point at which, five years into my efforts in community policing, the strategy clicked. It all made sense. And it could be done only hand in hand with those who have the most invested in a neighborhood—its residents.

CHAPTER 12

BIG-PICTURE POLICING

———

I T'S RARE THAT AN OFFICER IS CALLED IN TO SEE THE CHIEF unless there's trouble. So in 2005, when Chief Kunkle requested a one-on-one meeting with me, my first thought was: *What have I done that would warrant a lecture or a slap on the wrist?*

"Have a seat, Brown," he said as I entered his office. I lowered myself onto a chair across from him. "You know," he said, "my goal is to make this the best department in the country."

He cleared his throat. Not sure what to say in response or where he was going with this, I stared at him and nodded. "At this point," he continued, "we're still in last place."

I shook my head. It was true that though we'd made progress under Kunkle's excellent leadership as officers at every level generated a series of wins, we nonetheless had a higher crime rate than any other big city in the nation.

"We need to take our CompStat process to the next level," he went on. He paused, picked up his coffee mug, and took a sip while I tried to figure out what the hell he was trying to tell me. He had a reputation for being reserved, very cerebral, and somewhat aloof. This conversation seemed consistent with that.

"We need to be challenged," he told me. "Every one of us needs to bring our A game to the table. I want to transform this department and make Dallas one of the safest big cities in the country. This entire department needs to do better overall." *Good luck with that,* I thought. *Our unions, senior commanders, and good ol' boy rank and file will run you right out of town with your tail between your legs if you keep talking about all that transformation crap.*

Up to that moment, I'd never even considered what the "entire department" needed to do; like most deputies, I'd been singularly focused on improving my substation's area. As I listened, I wondered if he was trying to find a nice way to tell me that I was falling down on my responsibilities. The afterglow of my Operation Kitchen Sink victory had had time to dim. Maybe he was about to give me the boot.

"That's it," he finally said after ten minutes of talking. Feeling confused about the intent of the meeting as well as relief that I hadn't been canned, I rose from my seat, thanked the chief, and walked toward the door.

Just as I was about to exit, he called me back. "One last thing," he said. "I'm re-creating the second-in-command position. What do you think about that?"

I paused. The first assistant chief rank had been done away with years earlier. The person in that position was to serve as COO of the department and report directly to the chief, the CEO. The job also involved overseeing several assistant chiefs, which meant it could come with some unhealthy office politics; that was part of the reason the job had been removed. Billy

Prince, who served as chief from 1982 to 1988, had been the last to have a first assistant chief.

Upon hearing the chief's suggestion, I had no idea what to say. "I think that would be good, sir," I blurted out. "Maybe that person could help you meet your goals. I would encourage you to do that."

He smiled. "Brown," he said, "I'd like to promote you to that position."

I froze. I'm sure the expression on my face summarized for the chief the two words that popped into my head: *Who, me?* "Uh, that's going to be tough," I heard myself say before I'd even had a chance to think about it. "I don't know about that."

At that point, I'd been deputy chief for only a year, which made me a relative newbie at that rank. If I stepped into a second-in-command position, many of the assistant chiefs reporting to me would be more tenured than I was at that point. And though I'd served as lieutenant for five years, several officers on the team had held that rank for two or three times as long. I had my doubts about whether promoting me would go over well in the department—particularly since Chief Kunkle would clearly want me to hold officers' feet to the fire on their CompStat performances.

Despite my reluctance, he did not miss a beat before responding. "You're the man for the job," he stated matter-of-factly. "I'm confident in that."

One week and many hours of analysis later, I accepted the job—and from the start, as I suspected, the chief turned the day-to-day operations over to me. A one-year deputy. A once-judgmental ICP officer. A kid from Oak Cliff who'd never imagined he'd be second-in-command of a force in America's ninth-largest city, despite Walter's insistence. I was not only humbled by the assignment; I was very nervous. By then I'd worn my badge for more than two decades, many of them in a supervisory role. But I'd never led an entire department.

I would later learn that I had the citizens and city council members Blaydes and Griffith, as well as the Lake Highlands community, to thank for my promotion. After my team turned around that intersection, they'd done as they'd promised: They'd rallied behind me. At one point, residents and council members actually gathered at City Hall to advocate for me. Chief Kunkle heard them loud and clear—and he responded by offering me one of the toughest assignments in his department.

I WAS FORTY-FIVE YEARS OLD and twenty-two years into my career. My lightbulb moments up to then had, together, become strong enough to illuminate my path forward. The experience I'd gained at every stage of my ascent had given me the gift of perspective. A solid awareness of how crime fighting works on the ground. A big-picture view of what is effective, what isn't, and what lands in the middle. I'd also discovered that when you solve one problem, you can inadvertently create another. It's what sociologists call the law of unintended consequences, and it applies in policing.

Take, for instance, the illicit drug trade—a billion-dollar industry in our country. In the hierarchy of a dope ring, there are usually three rungs of distributors: the upper-level supplier, the mid-level supplier, and the street dealer. The upper-level supplier buys his drugs wholesale and then sells them to his mid-level supplier for a profit. The middleman, in turn, further marks up the price when he sells it to the street dealer, who will pay off the middleman with the profits he receives after selling to his clients. But when the police raid a drug house, as we did all the time when I was in SWAT, that street dealer loses his supply, either in whole or in part—yet he still owes a lot of money to the middleman, who will not take excuses in place of cash. So what does the street dealer do? He robs and sometimes even kills to round up money, trying to replace the cash and drugs that were recovered when the police ran their warrant. While the cops may have shut down an operation in the short term, they've also created the potential for more violence in the long term.

Our ultimate goal as officers is to nail the big-fish suppliers, not just the sellers on the street. But it can take years for an undercover narcotics agent to build enough trust with dealers to work his way up the chain and bust that ring wide open. In the meantime, the mothers and grandmothers who live near the local dope house can't safely walk down their block. They can't afford to wait for you to catch the high-level supplier because their quality of life has been significantly diminished. The big-picture strategy takes too long. So understandably, they call on the police department to implement an effective street-level strategy, even as the battle at the upper levels quietly rages on.

Yet shuttering that single drug house is like trying to close down one fast-food burger joint in a company's massive worldwide operation. Like the drug house, that restaurant is on that corner because a high demand for its product exists. And in order to permanently put it out of business, you can't just go in and remove all the hamburgers on the grill during that shift. That is a futile undertaking. All day every day, one shift after another, more burgers, bread, and pickles will be delivered. To effectively cripple the business, you have to intercept the product's delivery—the way cops have to uncover when and by whom drugs are being sent to a stash house. You have to identify the supply chain before you can interrupt it. And yet even as you work at that level, you can't neglect the legitimate concerns of the residents by failing to apprehend local dealers—even if that inadvertently creates new issues.

How? Law enforcement is complex, and its outcomes are mixed. By combating crime, you end up increasing it—true. We incarcerated people by the dozens, only to have them return to their neighborhoods and commit more crimes—true. And yet after we'd devastated a drug house, for instance, the law-abiding citizens in those neighborhoods at last had some peace, even if only for a few hours—that is also true and still a goal worth pursuing. So it's not that SWAT shouldn't serve its warrants. It's just that it'd be smartest to do so with the realization that that's just one part of the equation—the back end. And even as we're working at the street level, we have to diligently work our channels higher up the chain.

Here's another unintended consequence. The story of the 1980s and '90s is that our police department ended up blighting poor communities like South Dallas as we shut down (and in many instances bulldozed) so many of their buildings. The neighborhoods were reduced to empty lots and cement foundations with no structures built on top of them. And of course, we did not end the drug trade. We instead decentralized it. We pushed it into aging apartments throughout Dallas and out into the open air, on street corners like the one at Forest and Audelia. What was once done behind the scenes was instead done outdoors—in areas where criminals could sense cops were not ubiquitous.

As my time in Lake Highlands had shown me, hot-spot policing is one way to disrupt that cycle. The proof was in our statistics: By cleaning up that corner, we hadn't driven crime onto an adjacent intersection or street. We'd diminished it in every part of that neighborhood. It's not a perfect solution, because you can't wave a magic wand and obliterate violence. Wherever demand is high, particularly for drugs, criminals will always find a way. But in a profession with no black and white answers and plenty of gray areas, crime reduction is a much better outcome than lawbreakers gone amok, feeling like they own the neighborhood.

I CALLED A COMPSTAT MEETING—an accountability session for about thirty of our department's highest-ranking supervisors. It was time for us to get serious about moving the needle on crime reduction. From my spot at the head of the table, I made my way around the room, from one officer to the next. "Your burglary rate this month is higher than it was last month," I said to one deputy chief. He stared at me and nodded. "What are you going to do about it?" He laid out a plan that I thought sounded reasonable. "Come back in two weeks and tell me how it's going," I challenged. "And if it's not working, you'll need to come up with another plan."

Near the rear sat a senior commander reading a paperback. The more I talked, the faster this cop turned the pages. I could actually see the book's title and cover through my large-framed glasses; it was clearly a romance novel. And this wasn't the first time the officer had turned up at one of my meetings with a book in hand. I'd had enough.

"Captain," I said, "how many robberies occurred in your substation last week?"

A hush fell over the room as the commander looked up from the book. "I don't know nothing about nothing," the officer said defiantly.

"Well, can you at least tell us what chapter you're on in your novel?" I snapped. "Has he kissed her yet?"

Everyone looked down. It was so quiet you could've heard an ant crawling. "The next time I ask you a question," I said, "you'd better know something about something." I then proceeded with the meeting.

My response must've gotten everyone's attention, because that was the first and last time I was ever challenged in that room. Kunkle had hired me to play his bad cop so he could focus on managing city politics and the media. He hadn't had to explicitly tell me that he expected me to handle the operational side of our crime fighting efforts; I just knew. I also knew, from day one, that I wasn't necessarily going to be all that well liked after I began holding officers to account. That was fine. I've never cared too much what other people think of me; that's just my personality. If they like me, I see that as a bonus. If they don't, I'm still going to honor my commitments. I'd lost my closest friend and partner in the department seventeen years earlier, and after that blow, I'd focused on building my life outside the force: church, hobbies, friendships. I did feel a kinship with my former SWAT teammates, but the fact that I had no close personal friends in the department freed me up to do my job without conflict.

Yet while I was tough, I was evenhanded and respectful. Years before, during that eighteen months I'd spent in the 911 and Dispatch centers, I'd discovered how to bring out the best in employees. I recognized that others in the department were extraordinarily seasoned. Rather than feeling threatened by their experience, I sought it out and used it to our department's advantage. And as far as I was concerned, every officer's job was secure as long as he or she abided by the rules and showed marked improvement in CompStat numbers. Only the chief could do the hiring and firing, but I kept a close watch on who was and was not performing.

Some thought I was a quiet loner. The truth was that I, the boy who once stepped out boldly onto stage as Captain von Trapp, wasn't at all reticent. Who I was is who I've always been: Measured. Analytical. Intuitive. Calculating. The kind of child who once decided to give up football in favor of academics because I had the foresight to see where my road was leading. Yet I did not try to shift others' perception of me, because it worked for them to see me as reserved. This characterization allowed for a bit of the necessary distance that usually exists between a leader and his or her team.

FOLLOWING D.J.'S GRADUATION FROM high school in 2000, my son immediately enrolled at my uncle Johnny's alma mater, Prairie View A&M, just outside Houston. But the social adjustment proved to be a challenge for D.J., and after a year, he left school and returned to Dallas. I'd wanted him to complete his studies, knowing that would likely improve his earning prospects. Yet I understood that his path wouldn't necessarily resemble the one I'd taken. He had to find his own way.

Upon returning to Dallas, he initially shared an apartment with a friend while doing odd jobs to earn money. He eventually met his girlfriend, and in 2003, they had a son. Though he was grown and on his own, I was still hoping that D.J. would return to college or take up a trade. In 2007, he finally did.

"I'm ready to go to school," he told me one afternoon.

"Okay, good," I said. "Where do you want to go?"

"I'm interested in air conditioning and electrical training," he explained.

"That's excellent," I told him. "There's a lot of demand in that area. You could make a good living doing that."

I wanted nothing more than to see my son do well, and I offered to cover his tuition for a program at a local junior college and pitched in on rent for an apartment close to the school. After two years of training, he landed a job almost immediately. In the coming months, his life, much like my own, fell into the steady, familiar cadence of daily work and family time. That rhythm would soon come to an abrupt and frightening halt.

ONE EVENING IN THE FALL of 2009, my phone rang around midnight. When I picked up, I heard a piercing scream so clear and powerful that I bolted upright. "D.J., is that you?" I asked, still half-asleep. *Pause.* "Yes," he finally said. "Why are you screaming?" *Silence.* "Where are you?" I asked. *No answer.* "Stay where you are," I said, assuming he had to be in his apartment at that hour. "I'll be right there." I dressed quickly, and on my way out the door, I picked up my old King James Bible, the tattered and marked-up copy I'd had since before my son was born. I sensed I might need it.

At the time, my son and his family were living in Wills Point, which was more than an hour's drive from my place in Dallas. When I arrived, D.J.'s girlfriend met me at the door. "Are you-all okay?" I asked. "We're fine," she said, inviting me in. There, on the living-room couch, my son appeared totally calm. "What happened, D.J.?" I asked. "Nothing," he said, shrugging, as if he'd never called me. I went into my grandson's bedroom to check on him in his crib, and he was sleeping soundly. I returned to the living room to sit with D.J., and as we talked, he seemed like himself.

Then in an instant, his whole demeanor shifted. He began talking extremely fast. His speech, garbled and incomprehensible, grew louder and more rapid with each syllable. His body began convulsing, as if he were having a seizure. I dialed 911. Moments later an ambulance arrived and transported him to the hospital. The rest of us followed behind in my car.

While a medical team stabilized D.J., I sat, stunned and bewildered, beneath the harsh fluorescent lights of the waiting room. I didn't know how to begin making sense of what was happening to my son. I pressed his girlfriend for answers, but she was understandably reluctant to reveal anything to me without D.J.'s consent. I'd notified D.J.'s mother that he was in the hospital, but because of a long drive from her home to the hospital, she was not able to arrive right away.

"What's going on with him?" I asked his doctor. He cleared his throat and looked down at the linoleum, then back at me. "Sir," he said, "your son is not a minor. In order for me to share his personal medical information with you, he has to agree to it."

In the early hours of that morning, before dawn's first light, I sat alone at D.J.'s bedside. "What's happening with you, man?" I asked him. "What is it?" He looked straight ahead, expressionless, as if he hadn't heard me. "I'm just going to sit here until you tell me what's going on." Still he said nothing.

A short time later D.J. experienced another seizure. I called in the doctor, who again sedated him.

"D.J., it's me," I said after he'd returned to calm. "It's Dad."

"My name's not D.J.," he said.

I was confused and terrified. *What is causing the seizures? Does he have a chronic medical condition? Is he epileptic?* In all my years as D.J.'s father, I'd never seen anything like what I was witnessing. Not only was I afraid, I was completely in the dark. I opened my Bible and read several passages, printed in red ink, of words once spoken by Jesus.

Helpless—it is the only word that fully conveys what I felt that morning as I left the hospital. I knew something terrible was happening, but because I didn't know what it was, I felt powerless to do anything about it. And in place of an explanation, I carried with me a deep and abiding fear that I would lose my son. Through mile after mile as I drove home on the interstate, I prayed aloud. "Please take care of my son, Lord," I whispered. "I know we all have to go through difficulties, but don't let any harm come upon D.J." In the past, when I'd prayed for family, I'd often experienced a sense of comfort. During that car ride and in the days after, I felt no such consolation.

D.J. was released a day later, and in the months that followed, we seldom spoke of the incident. I didn't want to make him uncomfortable by prying. Yet as the father who'd raised and nurtured and prayed over him for twenty-seven years, I wanted to make things better. I wanted to transfer whatever burden he was carrying from his shoulders onto my own. "How can I help?" I'd occasionally ask him. "What do you need me to do?" He did not want to talk about it. I had to accept that I, the public servant who'd dedicated my professional life to helping countless others, could not rescue my own son.

CHAPTER 13

FOUNTAIN PLACE

—————

W E SPOTTED THE WORRISOME MESSAGE IN A CHAT ROOM in late 2008. Officers in our department, in partnership with the FBI's North Texas Terrorism Task Force, had been monitoring the chatter on an extremist blog when they came across a post that raised a major red flag. "Does anyone on here have an expertise in building a bomb strong enough to blow up a building?" a user asked. Our undercover officer, or UC, who was posing as a fellow user, responded and began an exchange. Investigators identified the author of the suspicious post as Hosam Smadi, a nineteen-year-old Middle Eastern youth living in Italy, Texas, a suburb about forty-five miles south of Dallas.

Months before, Chief Kunkle had hired an undercover officer to become part of our terrorism task force, who, from day one, was a hot property in the department: It's rare to find an officer who speaks fluent Arabic (which, incidentally, is an excellent case for diversity in hiring). Now we learned that our

Jordanian UC happened to be able to speak the same dialect as Smadi, enabling us to identify the region of Jordan where our subject probably grew up. We could not have orchestrated a more perfect investigative scenario if we'd tried.

Background checks on Smadi showed that he'd never been on any of our watch lists. He'd never committed a crime. Though he'd declared affection for Osama bin Laden, he hadn't interacted with a terrorist cell or pledged allegiance to an extremist group. If he was planning to act—and the FBI's team of behavioral therapists determined, based on additional posts about his intent, that that seemed quite likely—he would do so as a self-radicalized lone wolf. In order to apprehend him, we needed more information. That's where our UC came in. We decided to set a sting. We'd send in our officer under the guise of an expert bomb maker with no apparent love for the United States.

We knew we had to proceed with the utmost caution. The federal entrapment laws mandate that, when a UC is secretly trying to build a case against a would-be criminal, that officer cannot use coercion or other heavy-handed tactics to push the suspect into committing a crime that he might not have committed on his own. If our UC, for instance, seemed to be leading Smadi to blow up a building rather than simply following along with his plan, Smadi's lawyers could later claim he'd never intended to act. "It was all just talk," the attorneys could argue. "Your agent entrapped him." Around our department, we studied the rules and came up with what we thought would give us an airtight legal case.

Our UC kept in close touch with Smadi—first in the chat room, and then, after he'd built trust with him over weeks, by text, phone, and face-to-face. He had to pull off an Oscar-worthy performance to strike up a friendship that would seem genuine to Smadi, who, like many criminals, was suspicious of everyone and everything. During their in-person meetings, he did not wear a wiretap. If Smadi had detected it, that might've gotten our UC killed on the spot. Every time they met, the officer gathered as much information as he could, often following up with Smadi via text and email to create a written record of his intentions.

Smadi told our UC that he'd initially considered targeting Dallas/Fort Worth International Airport with a bomb. After giving it more thought, however, he said he'd ruled out that option because the airport's security was too high. And aside from his concerns about breaching security, he did not know how to build an explosive, which was why he'd asked for help in that chat room. At one in-person meeting, he made it clear that he'd identified a new target: the Wells Fargo Bank skyscraper at Fountain Place, an iconic sixty-story glass office tower in downtown Dallas. He wanted to imitate the 9/11 attack, he admitted—only instead of using airplanes, he planned to detonate a car bomb near the structural pillars and foundation of the tower's underground parking garage. "I want to be someplace close by, where I can actually watch the building fall," he told our officer. He also admitted the following to our UC, as was later reported by NBC News in Dallas:

God willing, the strike will be certain and strong. It will shake the currently weak economy in the state and the American nation because the bank is one of the largest banks in the city. . . . The bank has billions of dollars.

Let's say that the bank has collapsed and they took the money out. The losses will be excessive in credit card information. Millions of people would incur losses: unemployment, poverty, hunger, and a strike to the head of the government. . . . Of course, our joy will be in the success of this operation.

"Can you help me by building the car bomb?" Smadi asked our UC. "I can build the explosive," the UC replied, "but it'll be up to you to detonate it on your own." Soon after, Smadi purchased the explosive materials and gave them to our officer.

I'd been second-in-command for about three years on the day this intel reached my desk. "I think he's getting close to acting," I told Kunkle. "If we don't stop him soon, there's a chance he'll connect with a real terrorist and go through with his plans without our UC's involvement." In collaboration with the FBI and after extensive briefings within our department, Kunkle and many federal agents all the way up the command chain in Washington, D.C., signed off on our operation. The game plan: The FBI would build an authentic-looking fake car bomb, supposedly one that could be detonated via cellphone. If Smadi tried to set it off using the number provided, that would prove his intent.

On the day of the operation, our UC arrived at Smadi's home and delivered the faux explosive. They then drove to Fountain Place in two vehicles: Smadi's getaway car and a Ford Explorer loaded down with the bomb. Once in the garage, Smadi parked the Explorer near the pillars he'd identified ahead of time. He left the garage on foot, and a few blocks away, he got into the passenger seat of the second car. The UC drove them to a nearby location, from which Smadi could both ignite and witness the explosion. "You want some earplugs?" the agent offered. "No," he declined. "I want to hear it loud and clear."

Meanwhile Chief Kunkle and I, along with the FBI and task force teams, awaited word of the operation's status; the commanders on the ground were providing us with phone updates. "Where is he now?" Kunkle asked a SWAT sergeant on the ground. "He just left the parking garage," the commander told him.

The UC stood by as Smadi dialed the cell number, one digit at a time. When he put in the final digit, he looked up at the tower . . . he waited . . . and of course, there was no explosion. The cell number he'd dialed rang the SWAT team, who swooped in from nearby to take him into custody. Smadi barely reacted—his apparent stoicism likely masking a state of shock.

In court, Smadi's lawyers made the argument we anticipated they'd make: Our UC had goaded Smadi into detonating the bomb. The judge did not buy their entrapment explanation. Our evidence was clear and compelling, gathered with great care over ten months of surveillance that included more than sixty interactions. Smadi was sentenced to twenty-four years in federal prison. And we, the team that foiled a horrific plot that could have led to a second 9/11, had one person in particular to thank on the Joint Terrorism Task Force—a straitlaced Dallas police officer of Arabic descent.

I'D GROWN INTO MY ROLE as first assistant chief. As I'd taken on more and more responsibility for the department's operations under Kunkle's remarkable leadership, we'd seen a double-digit reduction in crime; our CompStat efforts were paying off. Away from work, I experienced a shift of a different kind in my personal life: Cedonia and I proudly welcomed the child we'd been longing to have. Our baby girl was as adorable as she was full of giggles and energy. On the day I first held her, she wrapped that tiny pinkie of hers all the way around my heart and hasn't since let it go. As a boss, I can be strict. As a daddy to a precious daughter, I am a complete softie.

The months and years flew by, as they do when you have a baby. Before I knew it, our sleepless nights with our newborn had turned into pizza parties and trips to the zoo. When 2009 rolled around, our girl was already a toddler. And I, someone who's always looking for the next challenge, started to get the itch. But there was only one place left to move—up—and the job above me wasn't open. Though Walter had talked constantly about one of us taking the top job, that was really his dream. I'd never yearned for it.

That is, until Chief Kunkle announced his retirement in November 2009. He'd spent twenty-eight years on the force by then, the last six as head of the DPD. He was generally beloved by the team, and under his direction, much trust had been built between our officers and the communities we served. We still weren't where we wanted to be in terms of cutting crime, but significant progress had been made during Kunkle's tenure—and so much of his success had to do with insisting upon data-driven policing. It was uncommon for a chief to stay in the role for more than three or four years; the job is that intense. Up to that point, he'd been one of the longest-serving chiefs since the

1960s. Before any tensions arose with politicians, he decided to step down on his own terms. I took note of his timing.

When I heard the news of his departure, I went from lukewarm about the thought of leading the department to asking myself, *Why shouldn't I apply?* In retrospect, I could see that he'd been grooming several commanders as potential successors. Though I was second-in-command, I had never assumed I'd step into the top job. For one thing, I brought a particular skill set to the table—and other commanders brought just as valuable but different skill sets. I think Chief Kunkle might've intended for several of his top-ranking commanders to one day compete with one another for the job. Fair enough.

I knew my weaknesses, and they were the ones I'd always had. I wasn't good at politics—and because I'd had a front-row view of Kunkle's work, I knew a chief had to be good at navigating the city's political landscape in order to survive in the job. Another weakness was that, on my way up the ranks, I hadn't developed strong relationships with reporters. Others in the department had. When there's breaking news around Dallas and beyond, the media shapes the narrative. As an officer, you may be doing great work, but if journalists don't see it that way, a different story will get told. And that means you need to build longstanding relationships with the press. I hadn't nurtured those connections mostly because, earlier in my career, I hadn't deemed them important. I thought my work should be more significant than the story. It is—but if an inaccurate story is told, it makes the work more difficult and sometimes even impossible.

Once Kunkle announced his retirement, the city hired a

search firm to begin identifying possible successors from all over the country. That's standard. The city also began accepting applications from internal and local candidates. I went back and forth about whether I should apply: One moment I'd feel strongly; the next, I'd be unsure. One reservation I had, aside from the politics, concerned the history of African-American chiefs in the department. There'd been one—Chief Terrell Bolton, who'd been appointed in 1999. But by 2003, he'd been let go—a relatively fresh sore spot in the department's memory. I wasn't sure the city would be willing to select another black chief. That was part of my hesitation.

I also thought the city might be ready to hire its first Hispanic chief, especially given that Dallas's Latino population had burgeoned to nearly 40 percent of all residents. That would be a historic move for the city. There were some very qualified Hispanic candidates applying for the job—I knew of one in particular in our department who would make an outstanding chief. *What would I do if I were in the city's position?* I kept thinking. The answer: *I'd probably go with a very qualified Hispanic.*

I talked it over with Cedonia. By this time, she had put in just shy of twenty years on the force. I'd logged twenty-seven years and was already eligible to receive full retirement benefits. We'd also reached our goal of a debt-free existence, and we owned our home. So I was where I needed to be financially—and that made the prospect of applying more appealing to me. "If I were chosen as chief," I told Cedonia, "the salary would be a bonus—but we wouldn't need it in order to live comfortably." That was important to me. A chief who desperately needs that paycheck can be tempted to compromise his or her principles. If I was offered the job and was later asked to do something unethical, immoral, or even illegal, I wanted to know I could freely and fearlessly walk away.

There was another question for my wife and me to consider: If I became chief, how would that impact Cedonia's career? The department's nepotism rules would prohibit her from working under my leadership. She'd have to resign. By this time, she'd left narcotics, where she'd been a senior corporal, and after a promotion to sergeant, she was reassigned to an administrative job. "If I don't get the job," I proposed, "then I can retire—and you can keep working until you reach the twenty-five-year mark. And if I do get the job," I told her, "you could transfer to a city job and then retire." She agreed.

But weeks inched by, and I did not submit a letter of application. *Should I or shouldn't I?* It was a tough decision, and I couldn't quite make up my mind. *Maybe I should just step aside and allow the Hispanic officer to take the job,* I reasoned. *That would be good for the department and the city. And that's probably who they're going to choose anyway.* But the more I tried to talk myself out of applying, the less comfortable I felt with the notion that I should sit on the sidelines. My potential to be chief should not be evaluated in light of a previous chief's performance or skin color, yet the reality was that it might be. I wanted to live in a world that judged me based on my merits. Based on my experience. Based on the value I would bring. In February 2010, after months of vacillation and just before the application period closed, I chose the world as I thought it should be rather than the one it often is: I submitted my application. I wasn't going to count myself out first; I was going to make them tell me no.

And no was an answer I was ready to accept. What I couldn't have lived with was not even making an attempt. I have never played the victim in any circumstance. And it's a cop-out to cry in your milk that no one gave you a chance because of your race when you didn't even try. That's not who I am. I am someone who makes my own opportunities. I am the scrub from Oak Cliff who always played to win, even when others counted me out. And I refused to quit in the fourth quarter, with two minutes still left on the clock. I refused to concede defeat—but I was prepared to graciously accept the outcome if I was not chosen for the job.

More than thirty officers applied. That number was gradually whittled down to a few finalists, and I was one of them. There were no written tests; it was all interviews. So I put on my Sunday best and met with city council members, Mayor Tom Leppert, and City Manager Mary Suhm, as well as with police associations and civics organizations. I made a presentation outlining my vision for the department. Residents also gathered to ask me questions in a roundtable format. The interviews were rigorous, and they continued for weeks.

Every candidate was under the microscope. Journalists reported on and analyzed our career trajectories in a very public and thorough vetting process. Each of us had to be evaluated by a psychologist for hours; the city wanted to be sure the chief was lucid, rational, and clear-headed enough to make important decisions under enormous pressures. I was also questioned about my personal choices. In my interview with Mary Suhm, she asked, "How would you resolve the nepotism issue?" I told her that I'd arrange for Cedonia to be transferred to another city department that could use my wife's security expertise. By April, there were five candidates on the short list, a couple of them Latino: two officers from other cities and three department insiders—me among them.

Though I'd been managing the department for five years, I didn't feel like a favorite. Mary Suhm did a great job of keeping us all on our toes. David Kunkle had made considerable improvements during his tenure, and the feeling among the city's leadership was *Let's keep that going.* But they weren't necessarily pushing for an insider. They were looking for the leader who could best take Kunkle's progress to the next level.

In advance of the final decision, I made peace with the result: Either I'd step into the most demanding job of my lifetime, or I'd retire in the city that has always been my home. For me, it was a win-win.

CHAPTER 14

D.J.

—————

WAS HOME AT MY CONDO ONE EVENING IN APRIL 2010 WHEN Mary Suhm called me. "David," she said, getting right to the point, "I am selecting you as chief." It had been a tough decision, she explained, given the number of highly qualified candidates who applied. And yet after considering who could best serve the department and the city, they'd narrowed their list down to me.

A tide of emotions swept through me. "Thank you," I said, laughing out of surprise. "Thank you so much, Mary." We scheduled a meeting to talk through compensation, and after thanking her once more, I hung up.

As I delivered the news to Cedonia, I repeated, "Can you believe it?" We embraced, and she giggled right along with me. It's one thing to consider the possibility that you'll become police chief of what was then the ninth-largest city in America;

it's an altogether different story to actually be offered the job. "Congratulations!" Cedonia said. "I'm proud of you."

I was astounded that I'd been chosen. Following my interview process, as day after day ticked by with no news, I'd convinced myself that I would not get the job. There were too many excellent candidates. Aside from that, Mary was also well aware that I already had more than enough years in the DPD to retire. I didn't need the job, which could've given her a good reason to pass over me. And in the end, I thought politics would win out. I was glad that I'd applied, but in private, I'd resolved that I probably wouldn't get it. *They're going to tell me no,* I kept thinking. And then, to my disbelief, I heard yes.

I was beyond ecstatic—and almost immediately, that elation morphed into gratitude and humility about the significance of the responsibility I'd just stepped into. I'd been selected, but this wasn't just about me. It was bigger than my personal journey. This was about rising up to be a civil servant who'd make my city as safe as it could be and keep officers encouraged while holding them accountable, even in the face of strong opposition. This was about honoring the legacy of my best friend, Walter, who'd once dreamed this dream for me, and my mother, who'd sacrificed so much on my behalf. This was about the generations of family members who'd come before me, forging their way without excuse, even beneath segregation's long shadow. Their path from the basement of Old Parkland Hospital had led us to this moment.

Proud—that's the emotion I felt once the awe of the appointment sank in. And by *proud,* I do not mean egotistical or arrogant. I mean the kind of pride that makes you want to rise up and work harder than you've ever worked in your life. I mean the kind of pride that compels you not just to meet expectations but to exceed them by all measures. I wanted to do right as much as I wanted to do well. I'd grown up with no connection to Dallas's power brokers, its inside network of movers and shakers. Yet Dallas had given me, a kid from the inner city, an opportunity to lead what was then the eighth-largest police department in the nation.

After I told Cedonia the news, I called my mother. Mom was happy for me, but her response was somewhat subdued. "You be careful, son," she said after congratulating me, in an echo of what she'd said when I first told her I was joining the force way back in 1983. "Everybody who says they love you don't necessarily love you. Everybody who's smiling isn't always in your corner." She wasn't trying to dampen my joy. She was doing what she'd always done best—centering me and anchoring me in the truth. I listened and took it in, because I'd lived long enough to know that when my mother talks this way, I'd better pay attention. She has a knowledge base, an instinct and wisdom about life, that I do not have—and that I need in order to keep my feet firmly planted to the ground. "Don't get too high on your horse," she concluded. "And always remember to pray." On that last point especially, I'd have to follow her guidance more than once.

I rose early on the morning of May 5, 2010—the day I was to be sworn in as chief. I'd already taken the DPD oath as a rookie cop, and it was not a requirement that I do so again. If I did, it would be a formality. I chose to take the vow again—as a reminder to myself of the laws and principles I'd promised to uphold.

As chief, I had the privilege of choosing the person who would swear me in. I chose Larry Baraka, the lawyer who once mentored me, not to mention cured me of any inclination to wear a leisure suit. Years after we'd worked together, he'd gone on to become the first black district judge in Dallas County and had since retired. He agreed to do the honors, and that was significant for me because of the role he'd played in shaping me. His investment, his time, his energy, his care—the same care that my public school teachers had demonstrated—had everything to do with my arrival at this juncture.

The public was welcomed to attend the ceremony, which was held in the media conference room at police headquarters. My family was of course there, including my mother, my brother Rickey, and my uncle Johnny. About three hundred community members and officers gathered to witness me raise my right hand and repeat the oath, which was in part: "I, David O. Brown, do solemnly swear that I will faithfully execute the duties of the office of Chief of Police of the City of Dallas, State of Texas, and will to the best of my ability preserve, protect, and defend the Constitution and Laws of the United States and of this State and the Charter and Ordinances of this city . . . so help me God." The crowd erupted in applause as Mom, Uncle Johnny, and Cedonia all beamed.

Right after I was sworn in, I gave a speech. I told those gathered that I saw my position as so much more than a post. "It is a high calling," I explained. I spoke of the standard of excellence I hoped to bring to the department—and the community policing I planned to expand in order to transform Dallas into one of the safest cities in the country. "I can't say enough how much I love this city, having been born and raised here," I said, later referencing the deterioration in Oak Cliff that had drawn me onto the force. "To the officers in the department, I commit my passion to you. I commit my respect to you. To the command staff, I will support you, encourage you, and lead and guide you to this excellence in policing that I speak of."

As I talked, I could not help but think of Walter—of all those morning conversations we'd shared before work, of the way he'd mapped our plan for moving up in the ranks and one day changing the face of the DPD. Though it was I who stood at the podium, my friend was there with me in spirit. Becoming chief had been his aspiration. And every May after his parting, when our department held its annual memorial of officers killed in the line of duty, Walter's name was called. He'd given his life to make our city safer. At every stage of my career—sergeant, lieutenant, deputy chief, first assistant chief, and now chief— I'd been acting in his name. When I looked out over the crowd that day, I thought, *Man, look what we did together.*

Even after I was sworn in, I did not know why I'd been selected. The good Lord obviously had a sense of humor. He also knew that on Father's Day, six weeks from the morning I stood there with my right hand raised, I'd live through the greatest tribulation that my job as chief could ever bring.

I NEVER ANSWER MY PHONE when I'm in church. So on Father's Day 2010, when my cell began to vibrate during the congregational prayer time, I pulled it out, glanced down to see a number I didn't recognize, and slid the phone back into my jacket pocket. It could wait.

After the service, I checked my phone again and noticed I had a voicemail. I played the message when I got home.

"Chief Brown, this is Chief Keith Humphrey from the Lancaster Police Department," I heard. "Our officers responded to a call to your son's apartment here in Lancaster. Everything is okay. His girlfriend decided to leave their place and stay overnight with her parents. I just wanted to give you a heads-up."

D.J. was twenty-seven at the time. He and his girlfriend and their son had moved to Lancaster, a suburb about seventeen miles southeast of my condo in Dallas. I'd talked with D.J. briefly earlier that week, and we'd made tentative plans to see each other on Father's Day. Amid the whirlwind pace of the previous weeks, I'd been missing him. After hearing the voicemail, I thought D.J. and his girlfriend might've gotten into an argument that morning. I dialed his cell.

"D.J., this is Dad," I said on his voicemail. "I'm just calling to see how you're doing. Please give me a call back when you get a chance." I didn't mention that I'd heard from Chief Humphrey. I wanted to give him an opportunity to explain what was happening, without me coming across as accusatory. That was around two p.m. As I waited for my son to return my call, I drifted off to sleep. It had been an exhausting week.

On that week leading up to Chief Humphrey's voicemail, a particular sermon was on my mind. My pastor has frequently taught from a biblical passage in which the Apostle Paul asks the Lord to remove an encumbrance, his thorn in the flesh. Paul makes his request three times. God does not say yes or no but rather He tells him, "My grace is sufficient for thee, for my power is made perfect in weakness." The Father doesn't take away Paul's hardship. He grants him more grace to endure it. I'd been holding on to that lesson. Months before, as I'd sat at D.J.'s bedside in the hospital, I'd said to the Lord, "Help me to accept whatever you have in store for my son." I prayed the same prayer on that Father's Day.

At my condo that afternoon, my cell rang and awakened me from my nap. I picked up without even looking at the caller ID, figuring it had to be my son. But upon answering, I heard an unfamiliar voice. The caller introduced himself as a detective with the Lancaster Police Department. Then without preamble, he said, "Chief Brown, your son is dead. He killed a bystander and a police officer."

The breath literally came out of me as my hands began to tremble around the phone. I wanted to speak, to ask the detective to repeat what he'd said in the hope that I'd misunderstood him. But any words I wanted to say sat lodged in my throat.

"Chief, are you there?" he said.

"Yeah, I'm . . . I'm here," I stammered.

"Right now I'm at your son's apartment complex," he told me. "I'm so sorry, chief. I just wanted to let you know. We'll keep you posted."

The room seemed to darken. My entire body pulsated with pain, as if I'd been jolted with an electrical shock. I somehow rose from the couch and stumbled toward the kitchen to tell Cedonia. I don't remember exactly what I said to her or how she replied. But I will forever recall that she embraced me the way only a best friend can. In each other's arms, we stood together and wept.

Almost immediately, both my cellphone and our landline began ringing nonstop. The first call came from Mary Suhm.

She'd heard about the tragedy on the news. After offering her heartfelt sympathies, she said, "You let me know what you need me to do, and consider it done." Soon after, my stepdaughter, D.J.'s sister, rang. "Is it true?" she wailed into the receiver. "Is it true that D.J.'s dead and that he killed two other people?" Through tears, I repeated what the detective had told me.

After that call, I stopped answering. Everyone from friends and extended family to officers and local news reporters wanted to express their deepest condolences and learn the details of what had occurred. But in my fog, I could not bring myself to speak; nor did I yet know the details of what happened. The truth is I didn't want to know. What I'd heard had already broken me.

Over the next several hours, the story unfolded piece by piece, each revelation more heartbreaking than the previous one. Unbeknownst to me, my son had been living with adult-onset bipolar disorder, a mental illness characterized by severe mood swings and a chemical imbalance in the brain. On the morning of Father's Day, D.J.'s girlfriend had called 911 to report that D.J. was experiencing an episode. By the time the Lancaster police arrived, my son had seemingly returned to normal. Even so, his girlfriend left the apartment with my grandson and went to stay at her parents' home. That's when Chief Humphrey rang me. Later my son's condition had apparently deteriorated, and in the parking lot of his apartment, he shot and killed Jeremy McMillian, a man he did not know. Residents heard the commotion and called the police. When Officer Craig Shaw responded, my son shot and killed him as well. Other officers arrived soon after, and D.J. was taken down by police gunfire.

I'd eventually learn that marijuana laced with PCP, which can trigger a bipolar episode, was found in D.J.'s system. I will never know the full story of what my son experienced in the years and hours before that day, but my guess is that he, like many people who wrestle with mental illness, had rejected his diagnosis and any medication prescribed to manage it. He then likely turned to pot as a way to self-medicate. I don't know how long my son had been grappling with bipolar disorder; nor do I know at what point he began using marijuana or if it was responsible for his seizures. I can only speculate that the episode he'd experienced six months earlier was in some way connected to his illness. D.J.'s girlfriend had witnessed him struggling. She later told me he'd asked her to keep his diagnosis private.

Over the next few hours, a flurry of questions reeled through my head. How and why did D.J. get a gun? My son had never been violent or owned a firearm. Why now? How would the families of Officer Shaw and Jeremy McMillian go on after such a sudden and inconceivable grief? How would my daughter, my grandson, and the rest of our family deal with the aftermath of this? There were no answers, which intensified my sense of confusion and helplessness. The only thing I knew for certain was that God was still in control and had not abandoned me. Nothing else made sense. My pain cut both deep and wide, growing more excruciating with every breath. Loss itself is tragedy; loss without explanation is pure despair.

The detective called me twice more that evening. "Do you want to come to the scene?" he asked. I declined. As an officer who'd investigated dozens of crime scenes during my early years on the force, I knew it was important for the detectives to follow protocol, regardless of the fact that my son had been involved. And beyond that, as a father still reeling from the fresh grief of losing my child, I didn't want to be there; I wanted to remain in my living room, down on my knees in prayer. As dusk gave way to sunset, Cedonia and I continuously pleaded with God to bring solace not only to us but to the families who'd lost their loved ones.

Before that tragic day, I thought I'd known anguish. I'd buried kinfolk, some who shared my bloodline and others who did not. I'd mourned for those who'd passed on and felt my soul crack open in the mourning. Yet nothing I'd endured compared to the misery I felt after losing D.J. Most of my interactions during that time are now a blur, but the raw agony of that evening is unforgettable. Heartache was no longer a metaphorical description but a physical reality. Every part of me, inside and out, literally ached. A moment of distraction would bring temporary reprieve, but soon after, a tidal wave of sadness would wash over me.

You do not expect to outlive your children. When the reverse happens—when you bury your own son or daughter—life's natural order feels cruelly interrupted. It awakened in me a sorrow so intense and unimaginable that it cannot be adequately expressed in words. The world stood still as I reckoned with my despair, my regrets, and above all else, a single haunting question: Could I have done anything to prevent my son from taking the lives of others and then losing his own?

As much as I hurt after D.J.'s passing, in those initial weeks I grieved just as deeply for the loved ones of those my son had taken. I felt as if my own brother or sister had died at the hands of my child. I met with both families and repeated the only words I could say, as inadequate as they seemed. "I'm sorry," I told them, my head lowered. "I'm so very sorry for your loss."

We planned the funeral. The visitation to the mortuary. The graveside burial. I walked through all of it in a daze, and I have no memory of long stretches of time. Cedonia encouraged me to rest, but I couldn't. "Can you give me something to help me get to sleep?" I asked my doctor. That evening I took two pills and got the first full night's rest I'd had in days. The next evening before bedtime, as I held the prescription bottle in my palm, I thought, *If I take these pills again, I'll be taking them for the rest of my life.* I knew I'd always need something to anesthetize myself, to escape. I put the bottle in my bedside drawer and never again took it out.

Two weeks after my son's funeral, I returned to work. Charlie Cato, my first assistant chief, had overseen the department in my absence. I will always be grateful for the support and kind words that he and so many other officers extended to me during that time. In the media, some had questioned whether I'd resume my role. I'd decided that if the City of Dallas's leadership allowed me to continue as chief of police, I would be ready to serve. Mary Suhm, Mayor Tom Leppert, and my friend and confidant Pete Schenkel indeed welcomed me back with encouragement, love, and unwavering loyalty. In spite of my devastation, I wanted to lead. Retreating from the world for months on end likely would've rendered me frozen in my grief. My sense of duty not only got me out of bed; it also began my healing.

Long before I took on my role as chief, I knew life through the eyes of a son. A brother. A husband. A father. Each of those identities had shaped me, turning me into the man I'd become.

I couldn't have known it on that day in 2010 when I took my oath to lead the Dallas Police Department, but six weeks later, every strength I'd ever relied on, every faith I'd ever clung to, would be tested. Years would pass before I understood that test—the loss of my beloved son—not only as an immensely painful trial but also as preparation for the road ahead, a journey on which I'd be called to rise time and again. That path I've traveled is far more than a testament to grace. It is its very definition.

CHAPTER 15

CHIEF VISIONARY

WITHOUT QUESTION, CHIEF KUNKLE HAD LEFT OUR department and city better off. In 2005 alone, my first as second-in-command, we'd spearheaded a community policing effort that resulted in more crime watch groups being formed and significant overall crime reduction. In the four years that followed, citywide crime fell consistently, and in 2009, it reached its lowest point in fifty-one years. Kunkle had also added more than seven hundred officers to the ranks and expanded our use of CompStat. He definitely made some strides.

And that made my vision all the more clear on my first day as chief: I intended to supersize the contributions Kunkle had made. I wanted to push us to the next level, starting with an increase in our community policing efforts and assigning more officers to those tasks. Given how I'd first protested my assignment in that West Dallas housing project, it's ironic that I'd since turned into an ICP champion. The explanation for my

180 is pretty simple: I saw that community policing worked. The statistics had demonstrated that. And in large measure, it worked because it involved engaging the citizens—in other words, getting them to partner with us for the sake of their protection. They were invested. My plan was to preserve and even deepen that trust. And above all else, my goal was to make the city safer.

When I stepped into the top job, New York City held the distinction as the safest large city in America. That was the result of the hard work by the city's formidable trio of leaders: Commissioners Bill Bratton and Ray Kelly and Mayor Rudy Giuliani. Their success gave me something to aim for, a goal. I wanted to make Dallas as safe as New York City. And though we'd come a long way under Kunkle, we still weren't where we wanted to be. In my early days as chief, a single question drove me: *How do we get there?*

I've always been more of a listener than a talker, which is why my time as chief began with paying close attention. I read everything I could about the tactics that other departments were successfully using. I, along with my command staff, attended conferences where big-city chiefs convened. We asked questions and tuned in to hear the best ideas, strategies, and practices that we could bring back to our own cities and adapt.

I studied even those tactics that had been outlawed, such as stop-and-frisk—the New York Police Department's controversial practice of stopping, questioning, and detaining people they'd deemed suspicious. U.S. District Judge Shira A. Scheindlin later determined the practice to be illegal. She ruled that the manner in which stop-and-frisk had been carried out violated the U.S. Constitution. It had become a form of racial profiling in which blacks and Hispanics were disproportionately targeted—a finding that, as a black man, I didn't need a ruling to tell me. I introduced the stop-and-frisk topic to my command team as a way of launching a robust internal discussion—about how we, as public servants, could make our city safer while also respecting the rights of those we were trying to protect.

During this exploratory phase, good ideas were plentiful. After 9/11, for instance, the NYPD had placed monitoring cameras in hot spots all around its five boroughs. This was effective in three ways: It targeted crime in the densest areas (and if a situation arose, cops could be immediately dispatched); it was budget-friendly (fewer cops on patrol equals less money spent on labor); and the recordings could be used for investigative purposes (if a crime took place in a monitored area, for instance, officers could go back and look at the tapes to identify suspects and vehicles). On corners like Forest and Audelia in Dallas, we'd been doing with patrol cops what New York had done with technology. People are expensive, and to manage current and emerging hot spots, you have to hire more and more of them. I wanted to leverage our use of technology in whatever ways we could, as well as strategically allocate our resources. Installing cameras was one way that I accomplished that; bringing in license plate readers (placed on light poles and in hot spots to monitor traffic violations) was another.

I wasted no time in implementing my vision, a large part of which involved dramatically expanding the city's community policing efforts. My team and I created a midnight basketball program for local teens and officers at recreation centers. We organized health and safety fairs to get citizens out and interacting with police, as I'd done during my assignment in the housing development. It worked. By maintaining close ties with residents, my officers were giving people the opportunity to be witnesses. They'd talk about things like who was selling dope in their area. Who'd just broken into the house next door. Who'd been congregating after hours and robbing passersby. In many cases, that intel led to arrests.

I also created Chief on the Beat. At block parties all over the city, particularly in hot spots, I'd show up as the star several times a year. We often held the gatherings in school gyms because I wanted to get young people involved—and for them to bring their parents with them. We turned it into a can't-miss two-hour social affair, with cotton candy, popcorn, hot dogs, a pep rally, singing and dancing, and marching bands.

In addition to Chief on the Beat, we initiated many other programs, including a neighborhood Crime Watch network; Coffee with Cops, a chance for neighbors to convene, in a casual setting, with officers in patrol stations; Blue in the Schools, a series of lessons, taught by uniformed officers in classrooms around Dallas, on topics such as managing peer pressure; and Police Athletic League, which exposed youth to sports, the arts, and fitness through leadership and mentoring programs such as the boxing club, midnight basketball, guitar lessons, girl empowerment programs, chess club, Bikes for Tykes, career day presentations, tennis, bowling, summer internships, and a youth choir.

As you can see, we focused much of our attention on youth. The marked increase in drug use and incarceration during the 1980s and '90s had coincided with failing public schools—and many of those problems have persisted. That's why I saw it as crucial that, rather than demonizing public schools, teachers, and administrators, we instead join forces with them. If we officers could go into classrooms and initiate discussions on topics such as drug use and peer pressure, we could get our children thinking about how they'd handle those issues long before they're asked to take the first puff or try the first hit.

The whole point of all these efforts is engaging residents, from the young to the elderly, in as many positive interactions as possible with the police department—and that can shift their view of local officers as partners rather than adversaries. The approach is proactive rather than reactive. It's about investing resources and developing ongoing relationships with residents, rather than just riding in, gun on hip, when there's a crisis to manage or a riot to quell. Every department still needs a certain number of patrol cops whose main job it is to answer 911 calls, but even those officers can be trained to incorporate community policing tactics.

As our programs took off, I looked for new ways to measure their success. I'm a fan of hard evidence. How could we be sure crime was falling as a direct result of our community policing strategies? How could we prove both correlation and a cause-and-effect relationship? That's where the University of North Texas at Dallas came in. Our department partnered with UNT, as well as with other nonprofit research foundations, to evaluate our efforts using scholarly research. The bottom line: Community policing had made us safer than any other measure we'd used. This wasn't some feel-good, mushy, hocus-pocus variety of police work. This was law enforcement at its finest.

———

SOON AFTER I WAS sworn in as chief, Cedonia transferred to the city's water department. There'd been significant homeland security threats on water treatment sites and electrical grids around the city, so my wife's expertise would have been useful in creating security plans.

Though she'd moved off the force, critics whispered nonetheless: She still held a police officer's license issued by the State of Texas and by the department I was running. So technically we hadn't sidestepped a strict interpretation of the nepotism rules.

"It's not worth it," I told Cedonia over dinner one evening. "Why don't you retire?" She wholeheartedly agreed; she'd been wanting to spend more time with our daughter anyway. In late 2010, a few weeks shy of twenty years on the force, she took off her badge. She didn't quite get the full pension she would have received by staying until twenty-five years, but as far as we were concerned, the pension she got was close enough.

COPS MAKE MISTAKES. SOMETIMES BIG ONES. And early in my tenure, a few of my young officers used excessive force. The incidents were caught on dash cam, which meant there was hard evidence of the violations. I'm not going to relitigate each case; nor can I because of the legal protections in place for former employees. But I will say this: I did not tolerate that behavior. It's neither honorable nor legal, which is why I took swift action. I was willing to give my officers the benefit of the doubt, because I know what it takes to do the job. But if there was proof of gross negligence, that was, in my book, the end of the story. That officer was held fully responsible for his or her negligence.

My response sent a clear message through the ranks: *You cannot be a public servant who abuses the very people you're supposed to protect.* Not on my watch. This wasn't about making heads roll just to prove I was the new big shot in town. As a matter of fact, ending officers' careers was gut-wrenching during the more than sixty cases in which I had to let cops go for misconduct. It was about creating an environment in which honor, competence, integrity, and excellent service carried the day—and dishonorable behavior was immediately addressed. In my department, those who followed the rules held on to their jobs. The handful who didn't had to go. The reputation of the majority of the officers who made us proud every day with their commitment and sacrifice would not be tarnished because I couldn't make the tough call.

Such a stance is necessary; in fact, it's critical to the long-term success of any police department. A few bad apples can shape the public's view of its law enforcement team. Tolerating illegal and reprehensible behavior diminishes the reputation of the vast majority of officers who do the right thing. Citizens will see those two or three corrupt officers as representational of the department. That is why those who don't play by the rules should be promptly dismissed.

I hired far more cops than I fired—and in so doing, I prioritized diversity. I didn't have a political agenda regarding race; rather, my choice to recruit more officers of color was based on smart business. It made sense for our department to reflect the community it served. Dallas is a majority-minority city that, in 2010, was more than 40 percent Hispanic. Yet before Chief Kunkle became more intentional about hiring Hispanics, they had comprised only about 12 percent of our force.

Such a disparity comes with major drawbacks for law enforcers. For one thing, cops often have to overcome a language barrier in order to communicate with crime victims and interview suspects. Furthermore, some members of the public do not feel an officer of a different racial background can adequately serve them. That is not true, but it is also beside the point. Their worldview has been shaped by how they grew up, what they've seen on television, and what they've witnessed in their communities. That perception has become their reality, and in order to reach them, an officer must remain cognizant of his or her lens on the world. The biggest burden often falls on the shoulders of white cops, particularly those who work in communities of color. The onus is on officers of every background—black, white, Hispanic, Asian, Native American, or otherwise—to come together to enhance our understanding of one another's communities, as well as our approach for rooting out criminals within them.

Diversity for diversity's sake is not a solution to anything. If diversity, however, can bring about improved relationships that lead to solving crime—and my experience had proven that it does—then I concluded that we ought to be more diverse. It was value-added. My goal was to turn us into a majority-minority force, and under Kunkle, we'd made progress. When I was second-in-command, our personnel division began recruiting more from historically black colleges and universities, and under Kunkle's direction, a Hispanic hiring team had been formed to recruit in areas all over the nation with large Latino populations. By 2010, the department had grown from 12 percent to 14 percent Hispanic. We remained a majority Anglo department—which gave me an opportunity to continue to push the boulder farther up the hill.

Community policing. Diverse staffing. Technology implementation. Building trust among citizens. Holding officers accountable. Time would reveal the full measure of the dividends to be reaped.

A WEEK AFTER I BURIED D.J., a dear friend made a comment. "If you'd lost your son two months earlier," he told me, "you probably would not have been appointed chief. God must have big things in store for you." At the time, I was walking around in a cloud of grief, still numb from the blow of losing my son. When I heard his words, I thought, *What does that mean? What is he talking about? How could the pain I'm experiencing be part of some grand plan?* I knew my friend was well-intentioned, but his words seemed almost cruel. Years would pass before I understood them.

I still don't know why God allowed D.J. to take the lives of others before taking his. Even if there were an explanation, it would likely do nothing to blunt the raw agony of it all. When I resumed my responsibilities as chief, I moved forward with an enormous hole in my heart. It is still there. And yet as I dove into my work, trying to forget what pained me so deeply, there were constant reminders in the work itself. Every time we dealt with a mental illness or gun violence case, every time I looked into the faces of young people battling addiction—in their eyes and amid their struggles, I saw my beloved D.J.

Before I lost my son, I thought I really cared about other people's troubles. On one level I did, but not deep down. The parents of the sons and daughters I came into contact with were someone else's sons and daughters. Their trouble. Their cross to bear. Their mess to clean up. Issues of mental illness, gun violence, and drug use had never hit home for me—until they hit my home. My family. My son. D.J.'s death began to make my work truly personal for the first time in a more loving way, as if the victims, suspects, and all the families were a part of me. I could feel their human frailty and their pain. I truly cared.

Another unexpected gift eventually arose from the tragedy—I emerged with a stronger sense of hope. Hope is not for the already hopeful. It's for those who are stumbling around in the dark, reaching for a faith to cling to in their hour of despair. In times of peace and serenity, we don't long for that hope in the same way we do when we're experiencing anguish. We don't appreciate it in its fullness. Before I lost my son, I didn't. But after he passed, that hope was all that remained—the only thing that kept me breathing. And I'd discovered it not in the best of times but in devastation. That is where hope lives: in the hard places, among the weeds, in the cracks. I had to go to the pit to truly recognize what I had. Not in month one or six or twelve after D.J.'s death but one breath at a time as I struggled to stand upright again.

A day when nobody is shooting at me is a good day. A day when no loved one passes on is a reason for me to whisper a prayer of gratitude. I've chosen to live in that space of thankfulness—and it is a conscious choice, because our default mode as humans is to dwell on what goes wrong. Rather than throwing in the towel on my faith, as I'd done after Walter's passing, I gripped onto it more tightly in the months after I lost D.J. That faith kicks in the strongest when you can't see your way clear. When your baby brother is gunned down. When you hang your head in sorrow for those who've died at the hands of your own child. I may never understand the good Lord's plans, but I do know this: There, in my heartache, He met me.

CHAPTER 16

PRESS AND POLITICS

———

HEN YOU SERVE AS CHIEF, YOU WORK IN THE SPOTLIGHT. Every choice you make, every word you speak, is scrutinized, as it should be. What you think you're doing in private on one day could become front-page headlines and water-cooler conversation on the next. That was why I knew I had to do my job by the book—particularly when it came to high-profile, politically charged cases.

Political tension is baked into Dallas's form of government. There are fourteen city council members, representing the city's fourteen districts; the fifteenth city council member is the mayor. Early in my tenure, that was Tom Leppert. When I took the job, I had the strong support of Tom and every council member; I'd worked closely with them as second-in-command, and there was not one dissenting vote. The council members and the mayor create policy. The city manager, then Mary Suhm, hires and fires all city employees. In turn, the council members can hire and fire the city manager and the city attorney. As chief, I did not report to city council members, yet they were effectively my boss's boss, and there were times when the politics of a situation needed to be carefully navigated—such as one that arose in January 2011.

On a Sunday evening when I was off work and relaxing, one of those council members called me at home. The fact that he was calling me during off-duty hours was not unusual: Council members often rang me anytime to invite me to holiday parties and other events in their districts. What made this call different was that it was personal.

"Chief, can you come to my house?" he asked.

I paused. "Why?" I said. "What's going on? Are you all right?"

He and his wife had just had a big argument, he explained. He sounded exasperated. He said he wanted me to drive to his home and help calm things down—an action I would never even consider. The last thing in the world a police chief should do is jump into the middle of a domestic dispute with a city council member. That would have been totally inappropriate, not to mention ill-advised.

"Here's what I can do," I told him. "I can send my detectives by to handle it. Or you can call 911."

He didn't seem to like the second option—and frankly, neither did I. On a Sunday evening, a 911 call would surely go to a rookie; new officers on the force were given the evening and weekend shifts, just as they had been when I first became a cop. A rookie typically has no clue about the potential media frenzy that could come with a high-profile case. Sending a rookie would be setting him or her up for failure, which was why I saw it as the least desirable alternative. So I was relieved when the council member agreed for me to send our detectives instead—senior, thoughtful, and seasoned officers who understood the political terrain and the role of the press.

Though sending detectives was preferable to sending a rookie, I knew I could be criticized for dispatching investigators. It might appear that I'd given the council member special treatment. After all, when an ordinary citizen has a domestic dispute, that person's only option for involving the police is to call 911. Yet on a regular basis, both while I was second-in-command and after I became chief, our detectives had been assigned to sensitive cases involving people of notoriety. I'd learned that it was wise to send in the A team to handle such scenarios, because when details surfaced in the press, the police department would almost certainly be hypercriticized.

"I'll send over a squad car this evening," I told him. I don't know whether he assumed I was coming as well. I was not.

When our call was finished, I immediately rang Mary Suhm, the city manager. I gave her the details of my conversation with the council member and assured her that I intended to handle the case by the book. She thanked me for notifying her. I then put on my uniform and went over to headquarters. In my office, I held a briefing with a special investigative unit of detectives, as well as their commanders. I recounted all that I knew and told them I was sending them in. "I want you-all to handle this case like you would any other—no favors," I told them. "And keep me updated." They agreed.

For an investigator, playing it by the book meant recording every interaction related to the case—which my officers did. When a detective first arrives on any scene, he or she has not yet confirmed who is a suspect, who is a witness, or whether a crime has even occurred. Only after we determine someone to be a suspect, who therefore has the right to an attorney, for instance, do we adjust our method of interaction. But initially, a detective makes an audio recording of everything for the purpose of documentation. (When a high-profile case hits the news, the details have a way of shifting, and it's important to have those audio files.) And of course, no citizen who has not been identified as a suspect has to talk to the police at all. Ever.

But this council member had a lot to say when the detectives arrived at his home—and he didn't realize he was being recorded. Officers are not required to reveal that they are recording their interviews. He spoke freely, explaining that during the fight he'd had with his wife, she'd pulled out a knife. She had then barricaded him into a room of their house, he said.

Those were his claims—and the job of my investigators was to attempt to corroborate his account with hard evidence. Otherwise, it's just one person's word against another's, and that does not hold up in court. "Did anybody see any of this?" one of the detectives asked. The man answered no. Though he was clearly worked up, my investigators reported to me, he did not appear to be physically injured. Detectives attempted to interview his wife, but she declined to talk, which was her right. With no witnesses and no visible injuries, there was no case. So my detectives did what they'd been trained to do: They created a police report and handed it over to the department, along with the audio recordings.

That might have been the end of the story—except that a journalist became involved. All police reports are public record, and reporters routinely go through them in search of news stories. I don't know for sure how this *Dallas Morning News* writer heard about the council member's police report—it could have been leaked. But once he got wind of it, his newspaper filed an inquiry, through the Freedom of Information Act, to review the full file—and by law, the information had to be released within ten days of the request. I'd seen this coming. I'd known since the evening when I'd got the council member's call that this revelation was probable or even inevitable. A story like this usually does not remain private. At that point, it had already become public knowledge, through the existing open record, that the council member had filed a domestic dispute; the newspaper's editors were just awaiting the full documentation and recordings.

I immediately informed Mary Suhm of the media inquiry. The city attorney, then Tom Perkins, was also notified, since all documentation requested through the Freedom of Information Act was to be released under his purview. I knew Mary and Tom would want to resolve this situation with the greatest care, particularly since the city council members had the power to take away their jobs. That was why I kept them fully posted on every move I made. And of course, in advance of the documents' release, I had to share the council member's report and recordings with each of them. After reviewing the material, Tom determined there was no viable legal reason for the records to be withheld.

In the meantime, the journalist who'd unearthed the report called the council member for comment. He denied that he and his wife had fought. In fact, he claimed he'd called in police after two of his buddies—he called them Arthur and Archie—got into an argument while watching a football game at his home. Our department released no statement. There was no reason for me to get into a tug-of-war about information for which I knew we had proof.

Just before the full recordings were released, Mary and Tom called a meeting with the council member. I was in attendance. They explained that the records would be revealed—and gave details of what was in them. I don't know if this was the first time the council member had heard about the existence of the recordings, but he acted as if it was. As Mary and Tom talked, he slammed his hand on the table and cursed in frustration. That week the council member challenged the city attorney's decision by hiring a lawyer to argue his case. But a judge ruled that the files, by law, had to be turned over.

Soon after, the full story broke. I chose not to make any public comment, either personally or on behalf of the department. The facts—which were clearly in sharp contrast with the council member's claim of a disturbance between a so-called Arthur and Archie—spoke for themselves.

The council member later told me he thought our call had been off the record—just between us. I, on the other hand, understood that the matter had automatically become public the moment he chose to bring it to my attention. As friendly as he and I had been, I had vowed to do a job, and if I'd handled the situation any differently, detractors would have rightfully accused me of a lack of transparency. If I'd learned little else as chief by then, I'd learned this: Trust is the most important factor between a community and its police force—and the only way to earn it is through complete transparency.

EVEN BEFORE I STEPPED into my job, I debated about the best way to manage the press. Kunkle's approach had been to grant special treatment to reporters from a traditional press outlet, namely *The Dallas Morning News,* which then had a content partnership with WFAA-TV, Channel 8. I ultimately chose a different, more democratic strategy: I would allow every media outlet in town the same level of access. It was part of my larger plan to give the public as much information as possible through every channel—from print and television to social media. My intent was to increase transparency by creating a level playing field.

That new approach did not go over well with reporters who'd grown accustomed to having the early scoop. For a 2011 press briefing at headquarters, I invited journalists from various news organizations, including a *Dallas Morning News* reporter. She was so agitated that she had not received an exclusive that, on her way out, she referred to me using two vulgar words— loudly enough for many in attendance to hear. She later asked me for a comment to use in her story, and I refused to give one. "I'm not giving you a comment after you've called me those names," I told her. She apologized and said she would tell her editors why I declined.

After the newspaper's top editors heard from her, they invited me to a meeting at their offices. The journalist herself was not there. "It's unacceptable," one of the editors said, "and we apologize." Fair enough. To their credit, the paper's editors eventually even printed an apology. Still, I stood strong in my position. I would not grant her or any other journalist an exclusive. It was not personal. For me, it was about adopting a winning media strategy at a time when print media was on the decline.

In the months after that incident, I shifted my focus onto an area that I, a fifty-year-old with a lot less hair than I'd once had, felt thoroughly inexperienced in: social media. In my day, in place of social media, my buddies and I traded stories and high fives on the sidelines of a basketball game. And to spread the word about an event, we posted flyers, not blogs. That was then. In 2011, though, millions of users across every continent were connecting through social media—and I saw the platform as an opportunity to communicate with Dallas residents. Without a reporter as a go-between. And with unedited content pushed out directly from the department.

That plan worked. We set up a department blog on which we shared everything from the press interviews I'd given to reporters (my team recorded the full questions and answers, to be sure nothing could be taken out of context, and then posted that online) to pertinent details of police-involved shootings, both current and previous. (I published twelve years' worth of Dallas's incidents; since there's no national database, researchers and activists, not to mention critics, had been requesting these numbers for years.) We put all these reports on our Facebook page as well: what happened, who shot whom, the race and gender of those involved, the outcome of the shooting, whether the officer was indicted, and if so, whether he or she was found guilty. Many applauded our new press strategy and transparency: The department won multiple awards from community media and policing groups.

At one point during Kunkle's tenure, a reporter had claimed

that our department was underreporting crime. That was patently false. But I didn't even need to have that argument: I posted all our annual crime reports for the world to see. No longer did we need to wait for our stories to appear on the noon, six o'clock, or ten o'clock news, or in the next morning's paper. We didn't need to rely on the traditional press to convey our facts and shape our narratives; the media has an important place in our society when it comes to informing the public, yet they needn't be the sole source of information. In real time, in our own words, we could send out our own accounts, which our citizens loved. Many responded by engaging in robust online discussions. Their posts, comments, and feedback drove the social media discussion—based on the accurate, unfiltered information we'd been able to provide.

It might seem counterintuitive, in a profession that often requires clandestine detective work, to go public with so much information. But even when a report doesn't make the police department look good—or perhaps *especially* when it doesn't—that organization's leaders are still out in front of their own story. They are not subject to rumors, gossip, and inaccuracies. And aside from that, if you cherry-pick your truth and withhold vital information about, say, a cop using excessive force, residents will assume you're hiding something when a similar situation later arises. Today's concealment could turn into next year's riot. The thing about trust is that it's hard to gain but easy to lose. I had nothing to hide, so I hid nothing.

I was on Twitter one day when I noticed a confrontational tweet from a *Dallas Morning News* reporter (not the one who'd called me vulgar names). I thought, *Maybe this is what Twitter is all about*—and I posted a reply for all to see. I wrote, in essence, that if I hadn't been cursed at, then maybe I'd respect the paper and the reporters it hires. My comment went viral. Networks picked it up. Activists, particularly African-American community groups, protested the fact that a reporter had hurled that kind of insult at me.

Mary Suhm's successor as city manager, A. C. Gonzalez, called and asked me to delete the tweet because of the language it included—and like a good soldier, I complied. I understood the pressure the city manager was always under as an employee of the mayor and council members. Though I hadn't appreciated being cursed at, I hadn't responded out of spite or retribution; I'm not a tit-for-tat kind of guy. I'd just wanted to experiment with using Twitter to set the record straight in 140 characters or less. Like all other forms of twenty-first-century media that our department had implemented, it got the job done.

THE CHANGE TO THE MEDIA landscape took place alongside another ground shift—in equipment technology. As a rookie, I'd shown up for work with only a holster and pistol, some extra bullets, and a baton. Today's officers start out with body cams and dash cams, as well as Tasers, which can eliminate the need for gunfire. When I began leading the department, I greatly expanded the use of these tools for one major reason: Research has proven that they can, in some cases, reduce the use of excessive force. That may not seem obvious in a world where officer-involved shootings have become commonplace in the news. But I suspect that such violations have always happened—and now that video recordings can be released to the public and widely disseminated via social media, the violations only seem more prevalent.

De-escalation of violence—that was among my greatest priorities as chief. Cameras and Tasers aren't just supplements to community policing; they *are* community policing. They are tools that can make the use of deadly force a last resort rather than a first one. The priority is to preserve life. Any nonlethal tool that can be used to make us safer should be used. And that includes holding officers responsible to the standards they've sworn to keep.

In my experience, not every rookie who makes it through the academy is suited to be a cop. Most officers are well aware of that. They know the cops they don't want to ride with. They're the ones who add fuel to any dispute that erupts, or start fights and escalate incidents rather than seeking to restore calm. They likely represent a small percentage of the force, but their behavior wreaks havoc for everyone else. That is why the bedrock of community policing has to be accountability—a fact I'd become painfully aware of a few years into my tenure.

An officer on my team once shot an unarmed black man. She claimed she'd done so because she was in fear for her life. But there have to be facts to support that claim. If a suspect surrenders—and in this case, an independent witness testified that the man had put up his hands—it is unlawful for a cop to shoot. Period. This officer was fired. The union protested on her behalf, but the termination stood. A criminal trial is still pending.

I took no joy in ending this officer's livelihood and career with the department, believe me. If union politics got me fired because I terminated an officer for shooting an unarmed person who had his hands up, then that would be a good firing. I could leave with my head up, my dignity in check. The law is the law, and as challenging and dangerous and messy as it can be to serve as a cop, officers must abide by the rules. When they don't, their peers and supervisors have to be the first to hold their feet to the fire. How else can we restore the public's faith in the vast majority of law-abiding officers who, year after year, bring great honor to this noble profession?

Never would that be more clear than during an incident in 2012—a situation that nearly made Dallas the first Ferguson, Missouri.

CHAPTER 17

DIXON CIRCLE

——

THE 911 CALL CAME IN ON JULY 24, 2012, AN AFTERNOON WHEN the temperature in Dallas had soared to ninety-seven degrees. "A man with his hands tied behind him is being dragged into a drug house by five or six Latino men with guns!" the unidentified caller told the operator. The location: Bourquin Street in Dixon Circle, a historically black neighborhood in South Dallas. Within seconds, two officers were dispatched with the emergency code that sends cops speeding, full lights and sirens, to an alleged kidnapping in progress.

The cops screeched up to the front of the house. They did not notice a kidnapping, but through the front window, they spotted a scene in the living room: a group of young men gathered around a table covered with illegal drugs and a gun nearby. Once the guys noticed the officers, they scattered in every direction. One of them grabbed the gun. The officers, unsure of who was carrying the weapon, bolted after them.

While some suspects slipped away, one man was apprehended in the front yard. Another led a cop on a wild and long foot chase: down the street, through an alleyway, over three fences. Several times along the way, the officer would catch up to the man briefly and engage in a physical struggle, but the man kept slipping away. After they'd leaped over the third fence, they ended up in a backyard barn stall, left over from a bygone era when residents owned horses. There they had a final fistfight, toe-to-toe and down in the dirt. The brawl, said a witness who saw it from her porch, was a pretty hellacious dustup. When the officer finally got the man under control and tried to handcuff him, the suspect grabbed the cuffs from the officer's hand and began swinging at him with the metal rings and kicking him in the chest. The officer, both exhausted from the foot chase in the heat and beaten down by the cuffs, would later tell us that he could not catch his breath and was about to pass out. "You're going to have to kill me!" the man yelled, according to the cop. The officer, in fear for his life, then pulled his gun and shot the suspect, killing him.

I was on vacation, just getting out of a pool, when a member of my command staff called me with the news. "Chief, we had an officer-involved shooting," he said, and rattled off most of the details, assuring me the situation was under control.

"What was the race of the suspect?" I asked.

"Black," he told me.

"And what was the race of the officer?" I asked.

"White."

"I'm coming to work," I told him. He tried to dissuade me, but I insisted. This was Dixon Circle we were talking about—a neighborhood with a history of heated reactions in the face of racially charged incidents. It was one of the few areas in Dallas where residents had protested during the 1992 Rodney King riots in Los Angeles.

At headquarters, as my team raced in and out of my office with updates, I turned on the television. Hundreds of Dixon Circle residents had already gathered in the streets. Newscasters and reporters, still trying to sort out what had happened, reported the main rumor that was circulating: A white officer had shot an unarmed black man in the back while he was running away. On television and social media, the speculation—in place of any facts—was taking root. I knew I needed an aggressive communications and investigative strategy if we were to have any chance of keeping the city calm.

I didn't know it at first, but the drug dealer in question was a kind of Robin Hood around this area: He handed out turkeys to residents at Thanksgiving and bought presents for children at Christmas. He'd also been a popular athlete at the local high school, and he had a large family and many friends living in the area. So when word hit the street that this man was the victim, what might've ordinarily been an impassioned response was shaping up to be explosive.

I fast-tracked our investigations. Under normal circumstances, it can take several weeks for a medical examiner to determine a bullet's trajectory: exactly how and where it entered and exited the victim's body. I did not have the luxury of waiting that long. "I want the medical examiner to get out there right now and look at the body," I ordered. I wanted detectives and senior leadership on the scene to observe the body and form their opinions about the case. "And get me a full pre-briefing of every piece of evidence you can find," I added. I then dispersed our full team of special investigators and key commanders to the location.

There they canvassed every inch of the scene—the home, as well as the barn stall and its surrounding areas—and identified and interviewed witnesses. That process typically takes two weeks; I wanted it done in two hours. Most newscasters had already broken in to their six p.m. programs with preliminary reports of the shooting, many based on the emotional accounts of loved ones and neighborhood friends who hadn't actually witnessed the skirmish. Before their ten p.m. broadcasts, I planned to be ready with some facts.

And that meant I had to take a calculated risk. Fast-tracking an investigation and going public with the findings left a good chance for the facts to change later. Most criminal investigations are fluid and constantly shifting, especially during the first few days. The full picture comes into focus only gradually, as the full set of facts emerge through disciplined police work. But as chief, I had to weigh the risks against the benefits in every situation, and in this case, I concluded that offering some information, even if incomplete, was preferable to having the press fill the vacuum with the only thing that existed at that point: uncorroborated reports. We'd simply have to preface our information with a disclaimer: "This is what we know right now, but the situation may change." We trusted that the public would understand that.

At the scene, my officers interviewed a credible witness, the elderly woman who saw the fistfight from start to end; the barn stall was in her backyard. She said the officer had shot the man as the suspect was beating the cop down—not in the back as the dealer was running away, which had been the rumor.

As my team gathered additional eyewitness accounts, the dispatch team and I carefully examined the taped 911 call for any clues. We were able to pinpoint the location from which the cell call had been made—another part of Dixon Circle—but we could not confirm the caller's identity. "Whose cell-phone is it?" I asked. Our investigators were already on it. One of the few providers that does not require its applicants to show ID or give a real name when they purchase a phone had sold the phone. As far as it's concerned, you can call yourself Daffy Duck as long as your money's good. And sure enough, this phone was under a phony name. Dead end—until we found the next way to search.

When the phone was purchased, a security camera at the store had captured the whole transaction. After combing that tape, we found an image of the person who'd bought the phone. It was clear enough for us to identify the man: a known drug dealer in Dixon Circle. By pinging the cell's exact location, our investigators found him, and within three hours of the shoot-ing, we took him into custody and began grilling him. His con-fession was full-throated and unequivocal: He, a rival drug dealer to the man who'd been shot, had made the bogus 911 call. He'd done so, he said, in retaliation. In a dispute he'd had with the deceased man some weeks prior, he had been beaten down pretty bad. The call had been his slick way of getting the man arrested. He admitted all this on tape.

Meanwhile the protesters—galvanized by the gossip that this dealer had been shot in the back, in cold blood, by a white cop—quadrupled in number. Their anger seemed to intensify by the hour, stoked by the flames of the false account. There they were, ready to burn down Dallas, based on half-truths and innuendo. Though we were still investigating, I wanted to release the evidence we'd uncovered as soon as possible—on the air as well as on our blog and Facebook page. I had to get out in front of this story before the lie fully took hold—before it reached the point where the truth no longer matters to many people. Like it or not, in the age of Twitter and smartphone news, the public often makes up its mind based on initial reports, even if those reports are erroneous. That's not fair, but it's reality, particularly in these times teeming with highly visible accounts of black citizens killed by white cops. We did not yet have all the facts—I was still awaiting conclusive evidence from the medical examiner—but we had better information than anyone else. If I waited two weeks to speak up, the city might be burned down by then.

I held a live press conference. During the briefing and Q&A, I did not hold back on the details: I gave the full names of the suspect and cop and a scene-by-scene account of the incident, based on eyewitness interviews. I revealed that the suspect did not have a gun. I also shared that the bogus 911 call had come from a dealer who'd been in a feud with the man who'd been shot. "We have as evidence crack cocaine in the house, in the front yard, and on the side of the house," I stated. I also explained that, contrary to the caller's claim, no Latino males had been seen in the house.

When a reporter in the press pool asked me whether the suspect had been shot in the back, I answered prudently but forthrightly. "Our preliminary belief is that he was shot in the stomach area," I said. "But that's very preliminary. The actual person who rules on where he was shot is the medical examiner.

We have to be very careful in determining entrance and exit wounds." Those wounds, as I'd learned during my time as a crime scene investigator, can appear remarkably similar. "We will continue to pursue the facts," I said. "The reason I'm doing the press conference is so that we can make sure that the neighborhood hears from the chief of police that I've been briefed on the facts, and I will continue to release information as we find out what's happened out there." I released the exact same information on all our social media platforms.

The residents of Dixon Circle apparently got my message. A short time after that press conference, the crowd disbanded on its own. Not a single person was injured; nor was there any damage to property. Our swift response and absolute transparency had prevented a riot—one that might have become like the violent protests to rock Ferguson, Missouri, two summers later after a white officer fatally shot Michael Brown, a nineteen-year-old black man.

In the aftermath of the incident, the lessons abounded—and so did the tactics I used to prevent such situations from arising in the first place. I increased our community efforts in every regard: more de-escalation training for my officers, more policies regarding when officers could chase suspects, and more overall transparency, as I posted all available information on the city's police-involved shootings. It was no longer just a matter of me wanting to be more forthright with the public. In a rapidly changing world where mayhem could be incited with a single falsehood, it had become a necessity. At a time when truth itself is under attack, our democracy depends on transparency—and so does every police force in the nation. And as we seek and find the truth, we must have the courage to stand up for it—not just when our officers show great bravery but especially when they make mistakes that disappoint us.

The Dixon Circle incident sparked a spirited internal debate among the officers in our department. As the situation unfolded, some of the old-school commanders hadn't agreed with my choice to release incomplete evidence. But in the absence of answers, even partial ones, who fills the void? The press does, and their reporting can be shaded by information provided by those who may have hidden agendas. Our society has an insatiable appetite for both information and misinformation, and even if those reporting do not have confirmed details, I've seen many willing to rush a story out just so they could be among the first with a scoop. To challenge this, police departments have to be forthcoming with what we do know, while admitting that the story may change. Better for a chief to talk than some knucklehead who has witnessed nothing.

The coming years would see a sharp uptick in the visibility of unarmed black men killed by cops, with massive protests erupting in response: Michael Brown in Ferguson, 2014. Freddie Gray in Baltimore and Walter Scott in North Charleston, 2015. Philando Castile in Saint Paul, Minnesota, 2016. And the list goes on. Each time I heard about an incident, I remembered Dixon—with gratitude that Dallas had been spared. And thank heavens that we didn't just have a near miss and move on, patting ourselves on the back that we'd done a good job in fending off a riot. We used the experience to reinforce our strong belief that holding ourselves and one another to the highest standard of accountability is our duty, our obligation to the public.

Yet I'm as aware now as I've always been that no amount of

training or accountability can remove officers' flaws and frailties. Humans—all humans, and especially police officers—make mistakes. They must often make split-second decisions in order to save lives, including their own. Still, when mistakes are made—the kind that clearly violate law enforcement protocol and endanger the public—police supervisors must have enough integrity and courage to identify and let go of the few who should not remain in our profession. Such courage and principle are necessary ingredients in maintaining an excellent force.

IN TODAY'S RACIALLY AND POLITICALLY charged climate, I often hear a particular question: *Are white cops unfairly targeting and killing black citizens?* Reporters, residents, colleagues, and friends have posed that question to me more times than I can count, and understandably so. In my view, the question, though usually well-intentioned, is divisive. No matter what answer I give—whether it's *Yes, I believe people of color are unfairly attacked,* or *No, I don't think they are*—I will alienate a large percentage of the very groups that desperately need to come together. The way that question is framed is one major reason we remain divided, and the same is true about a question I hear from officers: *Is there an organized community effort to ambush and kill cops?* In both cases, attempting a response will only lead you down a rabbit hole. It's not that we need to stop asking questions—it's that we need to pose more thoughtful ones.

When someone wonders aloud whether racist cops are targeting unarmed black men, they've skipped over mountains and mountains of issues to get to that one. In many urban centers where people of color reside, some of the greatest problems are failing schools. Waning or nonexistent mental health and drug treatment resources. An endless cycle of generational poverty. Disenfranchisement. None of those are policing problems. Rather than singling out the community's relationship with law enforcement, I think we'd do far more good by asking the kinds of questions that can lead to solutions. For example: *How can we turn community protesting into actionable change? How can we deliver results that significantly improve the quality of life for residents in all neighborhoods, including the most impoverished ones?* Those are questions and conversations that matter.

Examining particular cases of police-involved shootings can be a productive part of that larger discussion, as long as we don't use the specifics to claim unproven generalities. If you ask me, for instance, whether an officer should shoot an unarmed man in the back while he is fleeing, I will tell you no. I will also tell you that if he or she does, that officer should be fired, based on the policies in place in law enforcement. I will also tell you that the cop should subsequently stand trial. What I won't tell you is what the outcome of that trial should be, since in our system of government, a judge and jury have the authority to make that determination. Nor would I render the lessons or outcomes of that case universal by concluding that all cops are racist. Each situation is to be judged on its own merits, and for every ten examples in which a cop has been in the wrong—and without question, there have been many—there are ten other cases where the officer was doing his or her job by the book. Which of these instances should define a profession as racist or not racist? No one likes being stereotyped, not African-Americans and not cops. And here's a more important question: *What inquiries should drive and frame our society's collective discussion on improving our cities and reaching across racial lines?*

The answers are complex and nuanced. They cannot be boiled down to a ten-second sound bite, a seven-word headline, or a 140-character tweet, though that is exactly what the public has been trained to expect and what the media often goes in search of. These short answers are costing us. They are further pushing us into our separate corners. The longer answers—the ones I want to spend my energy on—can actually lead us to a better place. They can bring about viable antidotes for societal ills that our law enforcement officials—civil servants who earn an average of $60,000 a year—were never meant to address, such as mental illness.

It's a fact now acknowledged by many that imprisoning hundreds of thousands of drug offenders and other criminals during the mass incarceration of the 1980s and '90s was not an overall winning strategy for reducing crime—and many of those I imprisoned struggled with mental illness (more than 40 percent of federal prisoners are mentally ill). Once paroled, they'd return to the same street corners and apartment buildings and kept right on doing what got them locked up in the first place. Or if they tried to turn their lives around by finding meaningful work or by entering a drug treatment program, they found it impossible to get hired with a record, and they found drug treatment resources scarce, particularly in the most impoverished communities. Most did exactly what makes sense in the world of an addict, a dealer, or a mentally ill person: They went back to selling or using, sometimes both.

With the loss of my son, the issues of mental illness, drug

use, and gun violence became personal for me. Why is someone with a mental illness allowed to purchase a gun? How did my son even get a gun? I didn't give it to him. The only gun I kept in my house was the one issued by the department, and I did not carry it when I was off duty. I know barrels of ink have been devoted to the topic of introducing legislation that keeps guns out of the hands of mentally ill people; I also know that powerful lobbies and political forces have often brought us to an impasse. But wherever any of us stands on the topic of gun ownership and our Second Amendment right to bear arms as American citizens, I hope we can at least come together and agree on this: We need to close the legal loopholes in federal background checks that allow mentally disturbed individuals to purchase guns.

Knowing what I do now, rather than becoming an officer, I might have chosen to become a drug treatment counselor. Incidentally, I could have also studied to become a mental health professional, an early childhood educator, or a policy maker who fights for increased mental health and drug treatment funding. Policing is the back end of the equation. Police are called in when it's time to play cleanup, when an arrest must be made or a terrible situation resolved. But police cannot address what I see as one of the most significant issues in our inner cities: the *demand* for drugs.

When I first joined the force, I thought it was about supply—and to the extent that you could curtail that supply, I reasoned, you could restore some order. That is not entirely untrue, but that approach does not do anything to address the demand for illegal substances. The drug dealers exist only because their customers keep buying. What first drives people to experiment with drugs, and why do they keep returning? Aside from basic physical addiction, they keep coming back because, on some level, the drugs are working for them. They are meeting a need. They are blunting a pain that feels too overwhelming to contend with. Or they are medicating a mental illness that, in a world that still stigmatizes mental illness, has gone undiagnosed. There are as many other reasons and factors as there are people. When we help our family members, our friends, and our relatives cope with the extraordinary forces that compel them to use, we simultaneously keep our communities safer.

When it comes to drug use and mental health, as well as any of the other problems that plague parts of our country, we don't have all the solutions. In place of answers, it's understandably easy to blame those in the spotlight: cops caught on camera. When officers don't do their jobs, they should face consequences. When they use excessive force on anyone of any racial background, they should be dismissed from the ranks. When their actions have seemingly been driven by racial bias rather than by fear for their lives, they have no place in any department. I know I stand with the thousands of officers in my profession who will always condemn that behavior. And yet as indefensible and horrifying as such behavior is, it's not the source of the ills that afflict urban communities. It's only a symptom.

I do not pretend to know everything about these issues. I'm aware that I have enormous blind spots—that I don't know what I don't know. And yes, there are many things I've done and said that I wish I could do over, such as participating in the mass incarceration of thousands of urban youth earlier in my career. But from where I stand now, I do know far more than I did when I started out on this journey more than three decades ago. And from my place at the intersection of three communities—as an inner-city kid; as a black man, husband, and father; and as an officer who has risked my life alongside scores of honorable cops of all races and ethnicities—I am clear about one thing. We will make progress only when we set aside our assumptions and really start listening to each other—now more than ever.

YOU WOULD THINK A PLUNGING crime rate would always be good news—and overall it is. During my first five years as chief of the Dallas Police Department—2010 to 2015—crime didn't just spiral downward. Our CompStat data graphs showed that it fell off the cliff. When I requested a study to examine the source of the decline, the results demonstrated that community policing had been the driving force. Though we were still far from the safest big city in the country, we'd moved up from last to within the top five by 2015. Our crime rates had fallen to the lowest levels in fifty years.

That came at a price. During every single one of those years, I'd proposed a budget to the city manager, the mayor and city council members, and the budget director. As crime fell in the wake of our community policing efforts, it became apparent that I could manage the department's $400 million-plus budget with a certain number of officers—in 2010, that was nearly 3,700 cops. From a city management perspective, it was smart to redirect the dollars we might have spent on hiring even more cops instead on expanding library resources and hours, as well as parks and recreation programs. That also made sense from a law enforcement perspective, because every child who's in a library or rec center after school is potentially one fewer child who falls into crime. So I actually advocated for those funds to be redirected.

But the situation began changing in 2015. I was losing officers, many of whom left for higher salaries in the suburbs. I had maximized the number of officers I could assign to hot spots and community policing posts; there always needs to be a certain number of cops whose job it is to answer 911 calls. By 2015, I'd lost more than three hundred officers. Community policing had made us safer for five years in a row—but near the end of that five years, I noticed an uptick. And I knew it had everything to do with the fact that I was hemorrhaging staff.

"We can't make this happen without more cops," I pleaded to the mayor and the city council and city manager's office. "We won't have enough resources for the next twelve months." They heard me. But given that I'd somehow pulled it off for five years in a row, I had very little budget leverage. It was a tough case to make—and apparently, I did not make it strongly or convincingly enough. The fact that I could not persuade the team to allocate more money to staffing would come at a high cost—to the department, to the city at large, and to me professionally.

CHAPTER 18

HEADQUARTERS

———

SATURDAY, JUNE 13, 2015,

MIDNIGHT

MY WIFE WAS THE FIRST TO AWAKEN. "IS THAT SOMEBODY shooting outside?" she asked. I, half-asleep, turned on my bedside lamp, stumbled over to the window, and looked out over our condo's parking lot, then across the street at police headquarters. From that angle, I saw nothing but heard what sounded like a jackhammer. "Somebody's probably just doing some work on the street," I said. I returned to bed and nodded off. A short time later a thunderous reverberation jolted me from my sleep. *That has to be gunfire.*

I called my second-in-command, Charlie Cato. "Do you have reports of a shooting near headquarters?" I asked. He didn't. Around the clock, via text and email, my commanders and I received news of every critical incident in the city. There weren't any notifications in our in-boxes. "Let me call Dispatch, and I'll call you right back," he said. Less than a minute later he rang again. "Chief," he said, "someone is outside headquarters in an armored vehicle—and he's shooting."

I threw on my ballistic vest and uniform. On my way out, my young daughter hugged me tightly and said, "Daddy, please don't go."

"I have to make sure the officers and citizens are safe," I told her.

She said, "Don't hesitate to use your gun."

I laughed. "I won't," I reassured her, then bolted out the door and headed for the Emergency Operation Center (EOC)—the gathering point, ten blocks from my condo in the basement of City Hall, where the city's top officials convene during a major incident.

On my drive over, I rounded the corner closest to headquarters. There, on the street parallel to the building, a scene from *Rambo* played out: machine-gun bullets from a fully automatic weapon sprayed out from an armored car, one of the largest such cars I'd ever seen. Several dozen officers returned fire, ducking behind their squad cars for cover. As the bullets from their pistols ricocheted right off the armored vehicle, the machine-gun fire did not stop. My instincts told me to stay there and join the officers in the face-off. But as chief, I had to manage the operation alongside the mayor, the city manager, and the 911 and Dispatch teams. I turned past the vehicle and continued toward the command center.

A 911 supervisor met me at the door. "You're not going to believe this," he told me, "but we think the guy just called us from his cell." "Let's play it," I said. While I waited for him to cue up the audio, I ordered our SWAT teams to the scene. On the tape, in a rambling rant, the man lamented that he'd recently lost a custody battle with his ex-wife after he'd been arrested on a domestic violence charge. "You took my child away from me," he snarled, his words saturated with contempt. He blamed police for his situation, he said—and this was his way of seeking retribution. "I'm going to blow you up," he told us. The caller identified himself as James Boulware—a middle-aged white man who, according to our records, had indeed once been apprehended by our officers.

In the 911 Center, reports of gunfire flooded in, jamming the lines. The callers' accounts were all over the map. Some said they'd heard shots ring out from a second-floor window of a building adjacent to headquarters; others thought they'd glimpsed several shooters loading into the armored vehicle and sent us their smartphone footage. And like our officers on the scene, who'd been reporting to us even as they crouched behind bullet-riddled squad car doors, many residents believed there were multiple shooters all around the area. In an open field on a shooting range, you know exactly where a shot is coming from. But in an urban environment where the sound of machine-gun fire echoes off buildings, it is nearly impossible to identify the source and direction of gunfire. Even so, until I could rule it out as a possibility, I proceeded with the assumption that we'd been hijacked by a group of assailants, not a maniacal lone gunman.

Immediately I ordered commanders to various posts. One team evacuated residential buildings and a hotel in the area. Another searched for additional shooters who might be perched on rooftops or hiding elsewhere. Administrators had already been evacuated from headquarters. Just before the shooting began, a few had gotten up to take a break and grab a Coke, only to return to chairs pierced with bullet holes. In addition to aiming at officers, the gunman had shot up some first- and second-floor windows. If those clerks had been in their seats, they'd be dead.

During his 911 tirade, Boulware had claimed he'd planted bombs around the premises of headquarters, as well as at the northeast and northwest patrol stations. Upon hearing news of the shooting over the police radio, just about every officer on the force had scrambled to get to work so they could take part in capturing this guy. One cop, on his way in near the back of the building, had stumbled across a suspicious black bag in the parking lot. He'd almost tripped over it. Once he told us about his discovery, we put two and two together: This had to be one of the explosives Boulware had referenced. I took him at his word that there were others.

"I need a grid search of our entire parking lot," I directed. In such a search, crime scene investigators cover every inch of an area, step by step, as if there were visible parallel and perpendicular lines across it. It's a way to ensure that not a single spot or corner is missed. Detectives also combed the interior of headquarters, and I dispatched search squads to our other patrol stations.

As the shootout raged on, SWAT sent in a remote-controlled robot to retrieve the black bag we'd discovered. As the robot extended its arm and picked up the bag, the pipe bomb inside detonated, hurling shrapnel hundreds of yards in every direction. A nearby car caught fire. At the time, we thought the robot's touch had prompted the detonation. We'd later learn that the gunman had detonated the bomb remotely, from his cellphone while in the armored vehicle—and the bomb just happened to explode as our robot reached for the bag's handle. Two other locations at our patrol stations were searched, but nothing was found. That left us on edge.

Meanwhile the gunman slowly drove the car back and forth in front of headquarters. He'd peep his head out from a window port briefly, take aim, and rain down a hailstorm of bullets. Whether he was alone or with company, this guy had apparently prepared for this. It's all too easy to do in our country: buy an armored car online, then purchase enough firepower to produce major carnage. And man, was he loaded: Minute after minute, he shot without ceasing. He fired literally hundreds of rounds at our officers and into headquarters.

And then, at about one-thirty a.m., the armored vehicle took off down the street and around the corner. The cops scurried into their cars and followed him. An armored car is too heavy to travel more than about forty miles per hour, but because it's bulletproof, there's not much opportunity to stop it. (Shooting out the tires is the best option, but our officers hadn't yet been able to get into position to try.)

He rolled onto the I-45 freeway and headed south of town. Our officers stayed right on his tail in a low-speed chase, mile after mile, exchanging intermittent gunfire. Thank goodness the freeways weren't heavily populated at such an early hour. After we'd first realized the gunman was on the move, a county police officer we'd been in touch with called a local sheriff, who set up tire-detonation devices along the freeway. Some of his tires went flat. He could've continued on his rims for a while, but he instead got off the freeway in a suburb called Hutchins, about twelve miles southeast of Dallas. He ground to a stop in the vacant parking lot of a closed Jack in the Box. A marksman with a close-range view of the halted vehicle shot out the remaining tires.

A protracted gun battle resumed—and to be honest, I don't know how our officers survived. The gunman just lit up their cars with round after round of bullets for another twenty minutes straight. When there was a brief respite in the shooting, our SWAT team attempted negotiations for a peaceful resolution. Even in a situation in which officers are clearly under attack, the priority is de-escalation through nonlethal means. "Sir, drop your weapon and come out of the vehicle with your hands up!" a sergeant shouted through his bullhorn. No response—other than additional gunfire. This cat and mouse game went on and on: He'd rise up slightly, peer out the window for a split second, fire, and then crouch down as our SWAT team, with their heaviest artillery, returned fire. At one point, we thought we had hit him, but we couldn't be certain. Nor could we be sure there weren't others in the vehicle with him.

Back at the command center, I'd put our comprehensive media strategy in place—the first time we'd fully implemented it after Dixon Circle. In addition to disseminating ongoing reports to the press and through our social media channels, I'd dispersed—right alongside my command teams—six public information officers (PIOs). In a large department like ours, a PIO's full-time job traditionally involves handling press inquiries and putting out press releases. No longer. Rather than having my PIOs wait around for questions, I put them in front of the story. Directly from the scenes, they sent out real-time updates through all our platforms. They reiterated that our investigation was preliminary, with details subject to shift. Our message boards lit up with video clips from witnesses, accounts from passersby, and Twitter and Facebook commentary that began trending.

As daylight approached, I knew we needed to end this showdown swiftly—before unsuspecting Jack in the Box workers and local residents stumbled into the path of gunfire. I ended all negotiations and gave the go-ahead to the countersniper to take aim the next time the assailant peeped out. The sharpshooter aimed his .50 caliber rifle from approximately two hundred yards away, gazed through his scope, took aim, and hit the man in the head through the three-inch-thick windshield. The guy's body fell forward, then collapsed onto the vehicle's floor.

We could not be sure he was dead, which is why our officers took their time in approaching the vehicle. Before the SWAT team could enter, the car—chock-full of ammo and bomb-making materials—burst into flames. Boulware's body was eventually recovered, but no other remains were found in the vehicle. We never tracked down any additional assailants. In the end, there was no evidence to suggest anyone else had been involved in the assault.

I don't know if Boulware had been diagnosed as mentally ill, but he was obviously emotionally disturbed enough to launch an attack that could have left hundreds dead, particularly if he'd pulled the trigger during business hours on a weekday. I'm still grateful, as well as astonished, that not a single officer or administrator was killed or injured that day. We'd endured a crisis at headquarters—a harbinger of a horror to come.

———

SINCE MY SWAT DAYS, I'd been in an ongoing discussion with my buddies about breaching entryways with explosives. The slammer technique is effective, but it doesn't always work. In some cases, you can't get the rammer up to a higher-level floor in an apartment building. Back then, in the 1990s, we'd decided that using a C-4 detonation device to blow off a door was too risky, especially in an urban environment like ours; there could be collateral damage to neighbors in an apartment complex, for instance, or to bystanders and property. Too much of a potential liability. Yet the conversation continued—and the seed was firmly planted in my head. After I was promoted to lieutenant and moved on from my squad, I stayed in touch with my teammates. They told me they'd begun experimenting with explosive breaching, but only during training.

A few weeks after the headquarters debacle, some SWAT team members approached me.

"There's a school of advanced breaching in Las Vegas," a sergeant told me, "and we'd like to attend." He went on to explain that the course included a competition, during which teams of officers worked to be the first to breach simulated doorways.

"Man, we've been talking about this since 'ninety-three," I said, still not convinced it was worth the risk of collateral damage in a crowded city that had swelled to over a million residents. "I don't know when you're ever going to use that technique."

That's when the sergeant reminded me of a claim I'd made five years earlier, when I was second-in-command. Then, the

SWAT commanders had pressed Chief Kunkle and me to buy a .50 caliber rifle. Initially, I'd flat-out refused. "You're never going to use a fifty-caliber rifle in a city," I told them. But after the manufacturer sent them the rifle on a trial basis, they brought me out on the range to fire it. From the three-hundred-yard line, I positioned myself on the dirty grass, aimed the long rifle, and shot the target accurately, within a dime. The weapon was so powerful that, upon shooting, my body lifted from the ground. I was sold—which I'm sure had been the commanders' intent in urging me to try it.

"You were so sure we were never going to use that rifle," the sergeant told me, "but that's what saved us." He was right: During the ambush, the .50 caliber weapon had been the only weapon we'd had that was potent enough to penetrate the windshield of the gunman's armored car. The unfortunate reality was, the world was getting more violent, the criminals' weapons more powerful, and we had little choice but to keep pace. So based on their argument, I relented. "You can attend the school," I said, "but any plans for explosive breaching need to come through my office for approval." They agreed and gleefully enrolled in the program.

BY THE SPRING OF 2016, the increasing crime rate hit a dramatic peak: There'd been more than an 80 percent increase in murders compared to the same point in the previous year. I had my theory about what was behind the spike: Feuding drug lords were likely re-engaged in turf wars. But I couldn't be certain, and I didn't have time to figure it out. I needed all hands on deck to quickly reduce the numbers, particularly before the hot and humid days of summer rolled around. And particularly because I had far fewer cops in my department—more than four hundred fewer than I'd started with. Criminals take note when officers are no longer as present, and they respond by expanding their territory.

Without first informing the city manager and mayor, I upset the apple cart: I reassigned six hundred officers from their day shifts to evening, which is when most criminal activity occurs, and I gave them a two-week warning so they could prepare for the adjustment to their schedules. I also put them on nightly foot patrols. I knew it was a drastic move, but an 80 percent increase in homicides warranted an extreme measure. I didn't have the patience for a delay; nor did the mothers and grandmothers who lived in the areas most affected by the skyrocketing crime—they needed me to take abrupt and aggressive action. And if I'd announced my plans in advance, the process would have become mired in politics while the violent crime continued. Union and police association leaders would've protested vociferously.

And boy, did they. Just about every union and association leader in Dallas, as well as a couple of city council members, blasted me. They furiously protested the sudden schedule change for officers, most of whom had grown comfortable with their daytime hours. Some of this anger and resentment were left over from the time, a few months earlier, when I'd fired that popular cop who'd wrongfully shot an unarmed suspect. Few had approved of that choice, and in their view, the scheduling change was the final straw. Just months earlier they'd applauded my management of the headquarters melee; I'd of course passed on the praise to my heroic officers. But that brief moment in the sun had long since come and gone, and in March 2016, weeks after I'd announced the shift changes, the union presidents called for my resignation. Even some African-American unions that had always stood in my corner wanted to boot me out. They gave a joint press conference in which they publicly requested that I step down.

That stung, of course, but I knew it came with the terrain—so I took it like a soldier. From day one of the job, I'd had my critics, and no one has ever been harder on me than I am on myself. Rather than seeing detractors as enemies, I tried to learn from them. In every criticism lives a seed of truth that can lead to improvement, if you're willing to see it that way. So as a matter of principle, I did not mind that they were hammering me. But as a matter of progress, there was only one wise course I could have taken—and it was the one I'd chosen. If that would eventually cost me my job, so be it.

The phone rang off the hook, and I let most of the calls roll over to voicemail. Officers at every rank stormed into my office with their grievances. As the unions complained to City Manager A. C. Gonzalez and Mayor Mike Rawlings, they called me in to explain why I'd suddenly gone maverick. I had only one reason: "I have to get those numbers down." Cops are public servants in a 24/7 business, I reminded them. They're supposed to fight crime wherever and whenever it's most necessary, regardless of whether that's convenient for their schedules. My supervisors understood my view but were displeased that I hadn't notified them first. I sat there and nodded without much response. In retrospect, I should have informed them.

Then again, I didn't regret my decision to forge ahead, and within two weeks, our CompStat data showed a marked improvement. There was nothing more frightening to me than a double-digit murder rate going into summer. Not on my watch. Mike Rawlings issued a public statement affirming his support for my stance and declaring me the best chief in America. I will always be grateful for his loyalty and support during this difficult time.

Is the time nearing for me to retire? That question reeled through my head daily. The job of chief has a notoriously short life span for most, and after nearly six years in the role, I understood why. It's beyond intense. You're simultaneously under a microscope and inside a pressure cooker. I could handle the pressure. What I couldn't tolerate was leaving over an issue that, in the grand scheme of things, didn't seem important enough. If I was going to leave, I wanted to do so for insisting upon increased community policing. That legacy was worth falling on my sword for. But frankly, the backlash over shifting officers' schedules did not seem like a good reason to retire. So though I knew I was a marked man, I hunkered down. That was what Walter would have done.

In May 2016, three months into my sweeping changes, the numbers further improved, but not enough to meet my expectations. Meanwhile the public calls for my resignation had gradually subsided. Behind closed doors, though, those who'd been on a mission to oust me ratcheted up their efforts. I directed all my focus onto the most important task at hand—reducing the murder rate. In June, I assigned more officers to several hot spots around the city. And then July 7 hit.

CHAPTER 19

AMBUSHED

——

THE YEAR 2016 WILL GO DOWN AS ONE OF THE BLOODIEST in the history of American law enforcement. More than 130 officers had their lives cut short in the line of duty, and of those, 64 were shot to death—21 in ambushes. Cops killed 963 people, according to the *Washington Post* database. Most of those killings did not make national headlines, but over that summer, two claimed the global spotlight. Alton Sterling of Louisiana and Philando Castile of Minnesota were shot by police one day apart, just after the Fourth of July weekend.

Alton's death came first. On July 5, the thirty-seven-year-old black male was shot and killed after two white Baton Rouge cops responded to a call that a man wielding a gun was issuing threats outside a convenience store. Bystanders video-recorded the shooting, and soon after the ordeal, demonstrators gathered in the streets, shouting "No justice, no peace!" The following day, on July 6, Philando, a thirty-two-year-old black man, was pulled over by a Hispanic cop in a Saint Paul suburb. The stop turned deadly when the officer shot him at close range, as Philando's girlfriend, Diamond Reynolds, live-streamed the encounter on Facebook for the world to witness.

As news of the killings spread, tensions erupted. Activists had already banded together in protest following the 2014 death of Michael Brown in Ferguson, Missouri, and in so doing, they'd launched a national movement to make their voices heard. The Sterling and Castile shootings were just the latest in a series, and they served as a tipping point. Organizers encouraged citizens to gather in objection to cops' use of excessive force—and in memory of those lost.

That week thousands assembled in peaceful demonstrations in some of the nation's major cities. Atlanta. New York. Chicago. Philadelphia. Los Angeles. D.C. And of course, Baton Rouge and Minneapolis. On July 7, 2016, those winds of protest swept through Dallas. A two-hour gathering downtown was planned. As officers, our job was to protect our country's long, rich tradition of peaceful assembly while ensuring public safety for all those gathered. That Thursday we'd planned to do precisely that.

During the holiday weekend before the demonstration, I'd enjoyed a short time off. Nothing fancy, just a relaxing few days at home with my wife and daughter. I returned to work refreshed and ready to take on whatever the week would bring. I had no idea that that would mean surviving law enforcement's deadliest day since 9/11—a defining event for our department and for the city of Dallas.

———

MY TEAM HAD PREPARED thoroughly for the protest. During my time in SWAT as well as after I'd become chief, I'd managed my share of demonstrations, including the Occupy Dallas protest in 2011. In advance of every major demonstration, our officers initiate talks with organizers to gather information on, for instance, whether their event will be stationary or whether they're planning to march and, if so, along what route. After we'd had these kinds of communications with activists ahead of the July 7 rally, my team felt confident that the gathering would be peaceful. Organizers planned to hold their event in one place; there'd be a few speeches, and then the crowd would disperse. My officers and I had also tuned in to social media chatter to identify any potential persons of concern. Nothing we heard or read gave us reason to worry.

At the appointed time of seven p.m., a crowd of about eight hundred gathered at Belo Garden, a park at the center of town. My commanders and approximately one hundred officers were at the scene as I monitored the situation throughout the day from our intelligence center in police headquarters. In addition to following the news of protests in other cities, I remained tuned in to the police radio.

The Dallas event went exactly as planned, and those gathered were friendly and tranquil. It was a bit loud at moments—at one point protestors began chanting "Enough is enough!"— but that's common at a rally. As cops, we manage what I call "organized chaos" on a daily basis. That's our normal. Among the crowd, we had spotted about twenty activists wearing heavy SWAT-like vests, gas masks, and military fatigues. They also had AR-15 rifles slung over their shoulders. Though the presence of weapons certainly worried me—why would someone bring a rifle to a peaceful protest?—I knew the demonstrators had every right to display their guns. Texas is an open-carry state.

As the event was ending, the organizers made an impromptu move: They began leading the mass of demonstrators in a spontaneous march. Officers in squad cars and on motorcycles moved with them, some lining the route along Main Street. A few protesters stopped along the route and posed for selfies with officers. Meanwhile several cops leapfrogged ahead of the crowd to get to the coming intersections, so they could direct traffic and make way for the marchers. As they did so, they had to turn their backs to the crowd, a vulnerable position, especially considering they were clad only in their standard Kevlar vests—not the heavier additional ballistic ones. Yet my officers were out there doing what needed to be done, and thankfully rush hour had passed, so there weren't an enormous number of cars on the streets. The march snaked along Main Street without incident, and later the crowd began to thin out. *We dodged a bullet,* I thought as I studied the monitors. The gathering was ending peacefully.

I'd had a long day. By that point, I'd been on the clock for nearly fourteen hours, managing the usual department business as well as keeping an eye on this protest. I took one last look at the screens and decided everything looked in control enough for me to head home to my condo across the street. On my way out, I stopped in to see David Pughes; he'd recently replaced Charlie Cato as my second-in-command, after Charlie took a job in the suburbs. "Hey, listen, you-all just keep me updated,"

I told him. "And let me know when the very last person leaves the area." He agreed.

At home, I was just about to take off my uniform and hit the sack when my cell rang. I recognized Pughes's number on the caller ID and figured he was calling to let me know the protest had fully disbanded.

"Hello, uh—chief?" he stammered, sounding out of breath.

"What is it?" I asked, immediately sensing the urgency in his tone.

"We've got shots fired and three officers down," he blurted out.

That was a few minutes after nine p.m.—the last time I'd recognize my hometown as I'd always known it.

SOMETIME EARLIER THAT EVENING, as the demonstrators inched up Main Street, Micah Johnson, a twenty-five-year-old African-American army veteran, had parked a black SUV on a street near El Centro College and joined the crowd. He wore a ballistic vest and carried high-capacity bullet carriers and an SKS-styled semiautomatic assault rifle, yet next to the protesters with gas masks and AR-15s, he blended right in; no officer even took notice of him.

But unlike those others, Johnson went farther—bolting toward the intersection of Main Street and South Lamar. He charged up behind cops who were directing traffic and providing crowd control and mortally wounded three of those officers, without hesitation and in cold blood. "He's got a gun!" protesters yelled while running for their lives away from the gunfire. Panic ensued as people screamed and scurried in every direction. The shots echoed through downtown, the deafening claps reverberating from the tall buildings, making it sound as though the gunfire was coming from multiple areas, just as it had during the shooting at headquarters. Only the keenest ears and eyes could focus enough through all that chaos to determine that Johnson was the lone shooter, and several officers did in fact notice him firing and fleeing. With great courage, they engaged him in a running gun battle as they chased him into the El Centro Community College building. By this point, three officers were already deceased and others were fighting for their lives.

Cops in the area, not yet sure what was happening, searched for assailants amid the faces of the hundreds gathered. During the turmoil and confusion—and not knowing whether the protesters who had shown up with battle fatigues, gas masks, and rifles were involved in shooting officers—they showed the greatest discipline and restraint by not firing indiscriminately. Not a single shot was fired by officers at innocent protesters.

Meanwhile scores of officers and firefighters on the scene ran toward the gunfire. Others knelt over the bodies of their colleagues, desperately trying to revive them and get them into squad cars and ambulances to rush them to the hospital. When an officer is down, it's all hands on deck, so hundreds of cops were there, assisting protesters and evacuating all of downtown. Cops from the suburbs and neighboring counties answered the call and showed up in droves. Some of the protesters who'd been wearing fatigues and toting rifles were initially arrested and taken to jail. Once they were interviewed and ruled out as suspects, they were released.

Sirens screamed through downtown as ambulances rushed in

to reach those in need of urgent medical attention. Frightened protesters and passersby, all badly shaken, sought help and shelter wherever they could find it: beneath cars, inside the lobby of the nearby Bank of America building, crouched behind concrete statues and walls. Shell casings—hundreds of them—covered the ground.

PUGHES'S WORDS PIERCED THROUGH ME. "How many shooters are there?" I asked, my voice trembling as I rose to my feet.

"We don't yet know," he said. "There are reports of several."

"And what is the condition of the officers?" I pressed, my pulse racing.

"They're low sick," he explained—a term we use to describe victims who are not likely to make it. In that moment, I knew this was the most serious incident the department had ever faced. "I'll be there in a minute," I said, dashing toward the front door. "Keep me posted on my radio." Before I darted out the door, my wife and daughter hugged me tight, and we whispered a quick prayer together.

On my drive over to the command center, I rang Mayor Rawlings and City Manager Gonzalez and informed them of the shootings. They both rushed to the basement of City Hall. As soon as I arrived, I sent all our SWAT teams to the scene. "I want to hear the nine-one-one calls," I ordered. I instructed a dispatch team to report to the command center and run the incident dispatch operation from where I was seated.

The reports were streaming in by the hundreds, and as I'd come to expect, many of the accounts were conflicting. Some said they'd seen multiple shooters from multiple locations, both elevated and at ground level. With my blood pumping, I raced around to every area of the basement—from the 911 Center, to the situation room where the mayor and city manager and I convened, to the command center where our PIOs tracked the social media and cable news feeds up on an enormous screen. I wanted to hear and see everything firsthand, directly from the source, instead of filtered through others. I tuned in to the commanders' radio communications with one another at the scene, as well as the video clips and social media postings flooding in from those who'd witnessed the carnage. Trust but verify—that was my approach.

"Put the Facebook and Twitter feeds up on the big screen," I told my public information officers. "I want you to closely monitor everything that's being said—and immediately correct any misinformation." They leaped into action. The entire time I updated the mayor, the city manager, and the council members there, but I parsed my words carefully; I'd learned that a politician often digests information differently from the way an operational manager does. I thought of the family members and particularly the children of those fatally injured; these loved ones might have been en route to the hospital. The last thing I wanted was for them to hear news of their father's or husband's or brother's or mother's death before they'd been personally notified.

The sound of rapid gunfire mixed with shrieks and shouts came through, clear and unrelenting, on my radio. Large television screens in one of our conference rooms captured the unfolding devastation. Journalists, pausing as shots were fired, filed reports even as they tracked the movements of the gunman from their perches in nearby buildings. "Here comes someone running up and shots are being fired!" one brave reporter shouted. "I've never seen anything like this in my life."

THE ROVING GUNFIGHT INTENSIFIED. Several bystanders got caught up in the cross fire, and their wounded bodies collapsed to the asphalt. Inside the college building, Johnson fled up the stairway to the second floor. Officers briefly cornered him, but instead of giving up, he held them off with a volley of gunfire. At one point, he peered down from a second-floor window onto the street and spotted an officer courageously protecting innocent protesters. Johnson aimed, shot, and mortally wounded that officer. This was pure evil at work.

Officers who'd just reached the scene and hadn't witnessed Johnson escaping up the stairs understandably assumed there was more than one shooter—and that was the information they passed along to us at the command center. By this time, our SWAT teams were scouring every inch of the downtown area in search of snipers. "We can't find any other shooters," a commander told me.

Officers who'd been rushed to area hospitals fought to stay alive as their families were notified of what had happened. I disseminated some general information on the officers' condition, but out of respect for their loved ones, I did not share the full details. I also wanted to first personally confirm the reports of who had been killed. I held out hope the officers would make it and prayed to the Lord to spare their lives.

As tips surfaced, our officers interviewed person after person; more than three hundred witnesses would eventually be questioned. Many broke down in sobs during these conversations, utterly traumatized by what they'd experienced. The detectives, most of whom were themselves still in shock and grieving, maintained their professional composure as they recorded every detail of every story—then tracked down any evidence that might shed light on what had become the deadliest massacre in Dallas law enforcement history.

AFTER JOHNSON RAINED DOWN terror from his second-floor perch, the gunfire stopped momentarily. Officers who were already inside the building could spot Johnson looking for an escape route. He instead found a dead end, a blind corner he hadn't been able to see around from the entrance of the corridor. We'd later learn that there was a single doorway he could have fled through—and if he'd noticed it, countless more citizens and officers might have been killed. A small army of SWAT officers crept up the stairway and onto the second floor, first peering down the shadowy hall before shuffling toward the dead end. There, around that corner, stood Johnson, dripping in blood and sweat, loaded down with ammo. Our negotiations began.

"Put your weapon down and come out with your hands up!" the negotiator, Larry Gordon, yelled through a megaphone.

The gunman snickered. "I'm not coming out of anywhere," he blurted out. "I've already killed a bunch of cops," he bragged, "and I want to kill more. You dirty, racist police have taken the lives of too many unarmed black men. Now it's your turn to die. How many did I kill so far?"

He'd talk for a few minutes and then stop, peer from around the corner with his rifle raised, and fire at the officers. The cops crouched close to the walls and, holding up body shields, returned fire.

"The end is coming!" Johnson shouted.

"The end of what?" the officer asked him. In a situation like this, it is the negotiator's job to pull out information from the suspect and cool him off, all while distracting him long enough for us to gain a tactical advantage and end the exchange—whether through peaceful surrender or lethal force.

"It's the end for this entire city," Johnson responded. He claimed he'd planted bombs all over downtown Dallas—a message we passed on to our SWAT officers, who were already combing the area.

"Send me a black officer, you white idiot!" he yelled, clearly becoming unhinged. "I want to talk to a brother!" The negotiator who'd been talking was African-American, but Johnson clearly had assumed otherwise. We played along by pretending to switch negotiators. After a few moments, the same one began talking again, this time in a lower pitch.

"Do you like R&B?" he asked him, thinking that might convince him he was black.

"Sure do," he said. "I love some Michael Jackson." In between rambles, he belted out a couple of songs. This whole exchange was as absurd as it was terrifying.

"Yes, that's a good one," the officer said, egging him on. "Do you know any others?"

He mentioned a few additional hits, then returned to taunting the cops and assuring them he had every intention of killing more of them. As he bragged about the lives he'd taken, he also joked about his own death. It was clear he assumed he would not survive this standoff; nor did he seem to care. Dealing with an assailant who has little desire to live obviously puts officers at a disadvantage. And we already had one tall hurdle to navigate: We could not see around that blind corner to take a clear shot at him. "You're going to have to kill me if you want me to come out!" he yelled. "I'm never going to surrender!"

"Why are you shooting?" the negotiator asked. "What do you want?"

He paused. The response he finally gave still sends chills up my spine. "I want to kill white cops," he said, letting out a hearty laugh. "I want them to pay in blood."

CHAPTER 20

THE ROBOT

———

IDNIGHT CAME AND WENT. FROM HIS STAKEOUT DOWN a long hallway and around that corner, the assassin alternated between mocking officers, threatening to remotely detonate bombs, and firing at the cops in that corridor. He was determined to hurt as many more officers as he could, and as one hour of negotiations stretched beyond three, I knew I had to make the tough choice that only I could make. I had to end this horror.

"We need to do a press conference," Mayor Rawlings told me. I agreed. In preparation, each of my various teams gave me the latest: the condition of the wounded officers, the results of the search downtown for explosives, the latest eyewitness recordings, tips, and accounts. I needed every detail freshly planted in my head so I could deliver the news with confidence in its accuracy. I knew the mayor was right that we needed to update the public. The eyes of the world had shifted in our direction.

And yet the last thing I wanted to do was a presser. In a split second, this fool could charge down the hall and take more lives—and I had no time to be held up in front of a mic. I was already thinking ahead to the funerals of the cops we were going to have to bury, as well as the anguish of those who loved them most, their families.

On my way out to the podium, I talked by phone to one of the SWAT commanders on the ground. "When I get back from this conference," I told him, "I want to hear a plan. Use your creativity to come up with the best way to take him out." I'd concluded there was no way to end this standoff peacefully. Johnson had made it abundantly obvious that he was prepared to die and would never give himself up.

I stepped up to the mic and delivered the facts as I knew them. "At eight fifty-eight p.m.," I said, "our worst nightmare happened. Our Dallas Police Department and transit officers were fired upon. I am sad to say that we have deceased—and it is a heartbreaking moment for our city." Even after cornering Johnson in the El Centro building, I reported, we still hadn't ruled out the possibility of multiple shooters. No explosives had been found. With a cracked voice and lowered head, I at last delivered the most heartbreaking news: eleven officers had been shot, nine had been seriously injured, and three of those nine had passed on. "We're negotiating with the gunman as we speak," I concluded, "so I'm going to have to get back real quick." With lives hanging in the balance and anxiety filling every inch of me, I cut it short.

By this hour, my officers engaged in the standoff with John-son weren't just fatigued; they were borderline delirious. Like me, most had been at work since eight o'clock the morning before. And with their hands on their rifles and their hearts in their throats for nearly four hours, they'd been awaiting my go-ahead. From my SWAT days, I knew how frustrating and even infuriating it can be to wait. And wait. And wait some more for the negotiations to play out—and for your commanders to make a call. The whole time you're thinking, *What the hell is taking them so long? They're in the comfort of their command post while I'm in the line of fire.* It's the natural push-and-pull tension that exists between officers and supervisors. The adrenaline crashing through their veins initially keeps the cops on the ground dialed in, but as the hours tick by, they struggle to remain fresh and focused. And the longer they remain in that static position, at once exhausted and prepared to fire, the more likely they are to make mistakes. I needed to act—and fast.

"SO WHAT'S YOUR PLAN?" I asked Commander Bill Humphrey. He and I had been in SWAT together in the 1990s, and I was very confident in his skill level; he had the historical perspective that comes from decades of leading squads. He'd been at the scene the whole time as the terror unfolded. From someplace on that second floor away from the officers, he was whispering to me on his cell.

"We could charge down the hallway, confront him, and take him down," he said. I nixed the idea of a shootout right away. For one thing, that hallway was way too long. I had gone down many a long hallway in my SWAT days, and I'd always hated every step, exposed with no cover and nowhere to go. The corridor's walls were made of Sheetrock, which a bullet can easily penetrate. There'd be no protection for my officers.

"What's your alternative plan?" I asked Bill.

"We could hold up our shield as we approach him," he told me. Our department owned a metal protector made of ballistic materials. It was about three by five feet in size and had a bar across it for two officers to hold it up as they moved toward a violent suspect. I'd held that shield many times. Number one, it's very heavy, and I knew my team was tired. Number two, the shield does not protect every part of your body: your shin, your elbows, and your sides are exposed. If someone shoots you in the leg with an automatic rifle, you're going to lose that leg and possibly your life. I wasn't willing to take that chance.

"So what's your last idea?" I asked, running low on patience.

"We could use an explosive," he said.

I paused. Bill had been one of the officers who'd persuaded me to send men to that specialized bomb-breach training program in Las Vegas, following the gun battle at headquarters. He'd also been the one to convince Kunkle and me to buy the .50 caliber rifle.

"We have the robot here," he continued. Our SWAT teams had been standing by with a van filled with equipment and explosives; it had become protocol for them to arrive at the scene of every crisis. If we needed their tools immediately, there'd be no time to wait for them to arrive. "We could use our robot to deliver the explosive," Bill said, explaining that he'd already talked this over with our bomb technicians, and an ATF (Alcohol, Tobacco, and Firearms) team had arrived on scene to assist.

Up till then, we'd used our robot in two ways: first, to retrieve an explosive so we could safely dismantle it; and second, to deliver an item such as a cellphone onto the front porch of a barricaded person. Bill was suggesting we weaponize the robot by mounting some C-4 onto the clamp of its little metal arm. We'd then send it rolling down the hallway toward the assailant, as quietly as possible, and detonate the bomb. The robot—about three feet tall and two feet wide—was remote-controlled.

When it came to explosives, we'd only ever considered using them to breach a doorway or wall—not to take down a gunman. The idea of rigging a robot with a bomb had never been discussed, and it certainly hadn't been carried out in any police department in the country. I'd asked Bill and his teammates to get creative. This strategy certainly delivered that.

But it came with risks. Major ones.

What if Johnson heard the hum of the robot rolling down the corridor and lunged out to begin shooting again? Or what if the bomb didn't detonate? Or what if the explosion claimed the life of the gunman but also injured or killed nearby officers with its flying fragments?

"We'll use just enough C-4 to contain the blast at the end of the hall," Bill reassured me. "And we'll keep him distracted with conversation while we're sending down the robot."

"I like this idea," I finally told him.

There was a big chance that something could go very wrong, but I'd weighed that risk against the potential outcome: a decisive end to this ordeal that was least likely to get any more of my cops killed. "You-all work on that while the mayor and I go out to do another press conference," I told him. "When I get back, be ready."

Mayor Rawlings and City Manager Gonzalez wanted to pre-brief for the press conference we were about to hold. We gathered together with other City Hall personnel, and the mayor asked me for an update on the status of the operation. He wanted to know how many of those we'd detained were suspects we could charge; I told him we couldn't charge anyone. I could tell the mayor wasn't satisfied with my overall update and maybe sensed I wasn't telling him everything. He was right. The mayor then asked if we should seek out the help of the attorney general. "No!" I blurted out loudly. "I know what I'm doing." For me, this was a moment of truth. Would politics take over one of the most significant SWAT operations in U.S. history? Not if I had anything to do with it. That was why I didn't want to share all the options I was weighing to end the siege—for fear it would become politicized. Lives might end up hanging in the balance. No one in the room had any experience in handling this type of operation, but they were all very good at spin, better than me. But this was no time for spin. I cut the meeting short. "I'm ready to go out and give an update to the public, and I'll keep it short and accurate," I told them. I convinced the room to trust my judgment.

I tried to keep the second briefing even shorter than the first. That didn't work. The press pool was understandably eager for an update, so the discussion dragged on. In reality, it probably lasted only fifteen minutes, but it felt like forever. I felt so anxious that I could hardly even focus on the questions we were fielding.

Back at my post, I rang Bill. "Go take care of business," I said. He and his team had the necessary specialized training, and I had asked them to properly apply it. "Your plan is approved," I told him. "Just don't blow up the whole building. Call me when you're ready to roll."

———

AFTER THE PRESS CONFERENCE, the mayor suggested that he and I visit the area hospitals to check on our wounded officers and console the families of those who'd already passed. Before we left the command center parking lot, my phone rang. It was Bill. I stepped aside and took the call. "We're ready to go, Chief," he said. "Just waiting for your call." I gave him the final go-ahead. In that one moment, my thirty-three years of law enforcement—the training, the instincts, the experience on the ground—culminated. And it led me to the most important choice I had ever made as an officer.

When I hung up, I walked with the mayor to his car. I hadn't yet breathed a word about our plan. "We're about to end this crisis," I told him. "We're going to blow him up." I could see the blood vanish from his face as he gazed at me. I gave him a confident look like *Yes, I know what I'm doing*. I didn't explain the details, and he didn't ask for any. He could've tried to micromanage, but he didn't.

Mayor Rawlings and I were not personal friends. We didn't hang out or talk on the phone or get together on the weekends. But when it came to handling business, we were on the same page. I supported him, just as he did me.

BILL AND THE BOMB technicians prepared the robot—one we'd purchased back in 2008. It was the Remotec Andros Mark V-A1, manufactured by Northrop Grumman, at a cost of approximately $150,000. It weighed nearly 800 pounds. Its arms could lift between 60 and 1,000 pounds and could grip with up to 50 pounds of force. It came with a long detonation cord (almost like a long extension cord). We wanted the option of triggering the explosion either by cord or by remote detonation, the former being more reliable. My team carefully placed a single pound of C-4 in its clamp.

In the meantime, Larry, the negotiator, drew Johnson into a loud and prolonged conversation. "How are you doing, man?" he shouted. Johnson responded by belting out another song and spewing out a string of threats. Larry encouraged it. "I hear you," he told him. "So why is it that you hate cops so much?" That really sent him off into a full-blown tirade of curses and insults—which gave the commanders an opening to send down the robot.

The soft hum of the robot's motor was audible, but thanks to our negotiator, Johnson was utterly distracted, caught up in his own rant. He was trashing the police force loudly and blaming all his troubles on others. Through the gray shadows of the long corridor, the robot moved closer.

Just as it was within about a foot of him, Johnson peered from around the corner, spotted the device, and put his finger on his rifle trigger. Right at that split second, an officer triggered the cord detonation, and fragments and smoke scattered in every direction. A moment later a shot rang out. *Could he still be alive?* Once the smoke cleared, about ten officers crept down the corridor, hanging close to the walls, and rounded the corner. Johnson's body lay lifeless—charred, mangled, and bloody. He'd apparently had his finger on the trigger when the bomb went off, and it reflexively cranked off one last bullet.

It was finished. Finally. Our day in hell was over. At 1:28 a.m.

———

BILL CALLED ME JUST as the mayor and I were arriving at Parkland, the first of two hospitals we planned to visit. "Chief, we got him," he said, with relief in his voice. "It's done." I turned to the mayor. "The plan worked," I told him, explaining how we'd used explosives to end the standoff. He nodded, and in silence, we entered the ER waiting room.

About seventy officers and family members had gathered, their eyes bloodshot with exhaustion and grief. Many comforted one another with hugs. I hadn't planned to speak to the group at large, but I spontaneously chose to address everyone there. "This is a tough time," I said, extending my condolences. "We just used explosives to kill the man who we believe is the lone suspect. We have lost so many officers, and we're all heartbroken. We're going to finish clearing downtown today, but this is what I want you all to do. I want you to stay together. Don't let anyone divide you. Let's act like I know we can act under the most difficult circumstances."

Given the racial hatred that had apparently driven Johnson's murderous rampage, I sensed that my team could easily give themselves over to anger and begin acting uncharacteristically. That would be human nature—but it would also be unethical and unprofessional. So I wanted to plant a seed, to remind them who they were. "I'm a person of faith," I concluded, "and if you are as well, now is the time for us to pray." Many nodded in agreement. I offered similar words of encouragement and guidance when we arrived at the next hospital. Four officers were deceased, and a fifth was battling for his life. He would eventually lose that fight.

BY EIGHT THAT MORNING, we'd finished our search downtown. My team never unearthed any bombs; nor did we find evidence of any additional shooters. By this point, we were all running on fumes; most of us had been working for a full twenty-four hours. But in a crisis of this magnitude, sleep eludes you. When I returned home, I fell into Cedonia's arms, exhausted. She held me up and tried to comfort me, assuring me I'd done all I could do. "You need to rest," she told me, but I couldn't. I just lay there wide awake, still thinking about the families who had lost their loved ones in a tragedy that had shaken our city to its core. I was well aware that I had five funerals to attend. Of all my concerns, that one weighed most heavily on me.

Media outlets from all over the country descended on Dallas. My cellphone never stopped ringing. I was inundated with texts and emails from television and newspaper reporters. I decided to do one single and comprehensive cable interview, with CNN's Jake Tapper. Word got out. As I emerged from the remote location in Dallas where my CNN interview was filmed, I was accosted by reporters, asking me to comment or come on their shows. But I had to get back to work.

In the following days, the inquiries didn't dissipate. In fact, they ratcheted up. I wanted to address the media, but the feeding frenzy all but demanded a more organized response. Ultimately I chose to organize an orderly briefing, with the seating arrangements and number of outlets settled in advance. I set the tone that this was not going to be an out-of-control free-for-all. After what seemed like endless rounds of Q&A, the questions became repetitive. I concluded by saying that all future interviews and briefings would need to wait until after we buried our dead.

EVERY SINGLE ONE OF those funerals was filled with sorrow, heartache, and despair. I hadn't been personally close to any of the officers, but I was no less devastated on behalf of their families. Our entire department was. An unbreakable bond exists between officers. And when you fight side by side with other cops, when one of your teammates has saved your life the way my squad members once stepped up to save mine during the Arizona Avenue shooting, that bond is further cemented. Yet even among officers who've never met or spoken to each other, I've witnessed an instant camaraderie. A recognition. An understanding. A profound respect. Only the men and women who put on those uniforms every day to serve their cities can truly comprehend what it feels like to do the work that we do. And when we lose an officer, it is like losing a brother or sister. The wound is as deep as the bond has been unbreakable.

In the years leading up to July 7 and its cruel aftermath, I'd experienced what it felt like to comfort an inconsolable spouse. To tell an officer's children, howling and devastated, that their daddy is gone. To embrace a mother who'd just lost her youngest son. I'd walked through agonies that had turned my heart inside out, that made me want to pull the covers over my head and forever retreat from the world, and that drove me far away from God before ultimately bringing me back to Him. And when you've walked that path, you know what to say and when to remain silent. You know how to simply be present for the anguished amid their greatest despair, carving out the space for them to sit and weep. When I stood by the families of our fallen, I showed up with my full self, with all my heartaches, past and present. There was no script. My shoulder and my heart were what I had to lend. And it was my private grief, not my three decades in public service, that had best prepared me to offer the most meaningful consolation.

AS THE RESIDENTS OF DALLAS yearned for a return to normalcy, criticism surfaced about our handling of the crisis. A few questioned my use of the robot and C-4 to blow up the assailant— a method that had never been deployed in the history of domestic law enforcement. I had no hesitation about detonating an explosive. I had chosen against using a flash bang stun device, as some suggested I should have. That likely would have given the gunman a tactical advantage, a chance to hurt and kill more cops. He had already wreaked enormous havoc and bloodshed on my officers and was threatening to snuff out the lives of others. He never once showed signs of surrender. If I were presented with the same circumstances today, I'd make the same choice—without question, I'd do it again. It's easy to critique an operation from the comfort of your living room. It's an entirely different matter to be on the scene with your own life on the line.

Johnson was obviously mentally ill. His words and actions made that clear. I don't know whether he had any ties to an extremist group that endorsed the kind of racist rhetoric he spouted, but as he shouted his cries of revenge, he seemed intent on a sole mission: killing white cops.

In the stairwell leading up to the second floor, our investigators found the letters *RB* scrawled in Johnson's blood. Some speculated that the initials tied him to a hate group. Our investigators did not know for sure what those letters meant, but we did know this: He'd paused long enough, after murdering five cops, to leave behind a cryptic message.

In the weeks after the crisis, the residents of Dallas fully embraced our department and the family members of the fallen. Many offered to pay for officers' meals. I could hardly walk down the street without someone coming up to me, hand over heart and tears in their eyes, expressing gratitude and even offering a hug. What had been meant for evil had become good. Out of unimaginable sorrow and calamity, a sweet spirit of connection arose—even among those who'd never met previously.

PRESIDENT BARACK OBAMA ARRIVED in Dallas on Tuesday, July 12—five days after our city had been knocked to its knees. At a memorial service at the Morton H. Meyerson Symphony Center downtown, the president offered his heartfelt condolences to the grieving family members. President George W. Bush also extended his sympathies and prayers to those who'd lost their loved one. President Obama went on to address the country at large. "When anyone, no matter how good their intentions may be, paints all police as biased, or bigoted, we undermine those officers that we depend on for our safety," he said. "And as for those who use rhetoric suggesting harm to police, even if they don't act on it themselves, they not only make the jobs of police officers even more dangerous, but they do a disservice to the very cause of justice that they claim to promote."

In my remarks, I chose to speak directly to the families—

because I had actually worked with these officers. They were my teammates. They'd served, shoulder to shoulder, on my force. And their loved ones had become part of our department's extended family. As I'd been preparing what to say, a single word kept coming to mind: *love.* Across the nation there'd been so much tension between police officers and their communities. I didn't want there to be any question that our love for these men was beyond political rhetoric. Beyond whether they were Republican or Democrat. Beyond whether they were white or black. In the face of such abominable expressions of hatred, I wanted each and every family member to feel our collective care for them.

The one song that, for me, has always best described this unconditional love is Stevie Wonder's "As." I decided to use that song and its powerful message to anchor my tribute.

"When I was a teenager and started liking girls," I told those gathered, "I could never find the words to express myself." I explained that when I'd approach a young lady, I'd use a lyric as my opening line. "So for girls I liked, I would pull out some Al Green or some Teddy Pendergrass," I continued. "If I fell in love with a girl, I'd have to dig down deep and get some Stevie Wonder. So today, I'm going to put out some Stevie Wonder for these families." I recited the lyrics that had always touched me, including the one line that summed up exactly how I felt and what our city most needed to hear: " 'Just as hate knows love's the cure . . . I'll be loving you always.' "

I DON'T KNOW IF I've reiterated enough just how courageous and extraordinarily professional our officers were during the blow that shook Dallas. I am still amazed at how the servants of the Dallas Police Department conducted themselves. How each of them, in the midst of unthinkable tragedy, often while holding their fellow officers' bodies in their arms as they lay dying, rose up and extended themselves to the residents and marchers who needed them. In my three decades on the force, I had never witnessed such remarkable bravery. Such selflessness. Such heroism.

From the first time I'd heard that Stevie Wonder song back in 1976, it struck a chord with me. And for many years since, I've held on to that message. Because if you and I could just close our eyes and get past culture and race and socioeconomic status and the scores of other identity markers we often use to separate ourselves from one another, we'd recognize that we are all the same. That when you set aside skin color and political persuasion, country of origin and ethnicity, far more binds us together than disconnects us. Our frailties, our hopes, and our hearts are what unite us in a common humanity.

CHAPTER 21

HEART STRONG

———

"Grace tried is better than grace, and more than grace;
it is glory in its infancy."

—SAMUEL RUTHERFORD

A POLICE CHIEF IS NOT MEANT TO BE A CELEBRITY. AS THE dust settled on the July 7 crisis, the loud calls for my resignation transformed into a constant flow of accolades for the leadership I'd provided during the bloodiest twenty-four hours in Dallas's history. Those who had determined to push me out of my job hailed me as a warrior. Public officials and citizens alike approached me with heartfelt gratitude. One gentleman came up to me while I was having lunch. "Chief, you're my hero," he told me. "I really appreciate your sacrifice for our city."

Cedonia and I, who'd been bracing for months to be run out

of town, were touched to our core by the outpouring of love and gratitude. It all felt so validating, though of course, we were nonetheless heartbroken and reeling about the officers lost. As my notoriety reached an all-time peak, a realization set in: I needed to step aside. A great chief should never be beyond criticism. There shouldn't be a permanent halo over his or her head.

My wife and I began discussing my retirement. "This high cannot last—it's unsustainable," I told Cedonia. She whole-heartedly agreed. And the truth was, I had zero desire to go back to facing the harsh headlines or the general spirit of mean-ness that can sometimes come from police union bosses, report-ers, and council members. You can't be an excellent chief and consider yourself untouchable, bulletproof to criticism. I wasn't yet feeling that way, but I knew that could become my reality. The very nature of the job is to stand, tall and ready, to handle the inevitable incoming fire, all the while maintaining compo-sure and respectability. If I got too comfortable with all the praise, I could see myself potentially popping off at the mouth with something smart in response to an unfair critique. I'd risk acting unprofessionally or out of character. And that meant it was time for me to go. I'd spent my entire adult lifetime in ser-vice, six of them in the top job, and I felt fulfilled in my work. So in October 2016, after thirty-three years on the force and as Dallas's longest-serving police chief in modern history, I re-tired.

Leaving the department was an emotional roller coaster for me. I knew I'd made the right choice, but it was still tough to walk away. When you've put on that navy blue uniform and badge just about every day for three decades straight, policing becomes part of your identity. It grounds you. It fills you with a sense of purpose. It connects you to the other brothers and sisters who've courageously navigated that journey alongside you. And as chief, as much as I was able to accomplish, there were still a few things I wished I could've gotten done—like securing the funding to create an urban training facility where our officers could more efficiently prepare to fight crime in a city environment.

And yet as I tearfully stepped down, I felt grateful to have built a legacy that I hope will live on long beyond my tenure. When I became chief in 2010, approximately 14 percent of our force was Hispanic and about 20 percent was black. By the time I retired six years later, the department had become over 20 percent Hispanic and 25 percent black, and another 6 percent were from other minority ethnic groups. For the first time in Dallas's history, we had a majority-minority force—a reflection of the majority-minority makeup of the city's residents.

There were other achievements to be proud of. Between 2010 and 2016, with the help of my extraordinary team, we reduced the city's overall crime rate to its lowest in more than fifty years. That had everything to do with the widespread community policing initiatives and practices we put in place. I, the "lock 'em up" lieutenant who had once pitched a fit when I was assigned to bring community policing to the projects, turned out to be one of the method's most vocal champions. I took up the cause for a singular reason: It works. No other measure or tactic I'd ever implemented did more to make Dallas residents safe.

As the world turned its attention to Dallas during and after the events of July 7, I'm proud that our department was recognized as a leader in community policing. The president and federal officials called us a model. But I did not want the story to end there. I hoped that other departments around the country would borrow the strategies that had worked in our city, as well as pioneer new approaches. There is always room for improvement, growth, and innovation that can effectively slash crime and create a sense of connectedness in our neighborhoods.

In one of my final press briefings a few days after the July 7 ambush, I extended an invitation to those who might consider making the choice I once made to join the force and fight Oak Cliff's crack epidemic. When a reporter asked me what advice I'd give to young people, I said, "We're hiring. Get off that protest line and put an application in, and we'll put you in your neighborhood, and we will help you resolve some of the problems you're protesting about." After that comment, there was a 243 percent increase in applications to the DPD. To this day, I still mean what I said. Peaceful protest is an important part of our democracy, and yet service is the highest and greatest form of protest. To produce change, you must be willing to put some skin in the game. And no one can help you better than yourself and your own community.

RIGHT AFTER I RETIRED, my family took a much-needed vacation to Hawaii, then to New York. We unplugged from email and social media and just enjoyed one another's company, with no thought of plans for the next day or the following one. I was just thankful that the good Lord had allowed me to reach this point—the end of a long and satisfying career in law enforcement.

Retirement has given me the time and space to further reflect on my beloved D.J.'s passing. I still miss my son every day. That will never change. What has shifted, a little at a time, is my view of the loss. After burying my son, I grappled with the questions that such tremendous grief would trigger for just about anyone. *Lord, why did this happen to my family? And why did You allow my son to take the lives of two others?* When I returned to work following the funeral, a chaplain in the Lancaster Police Department said to me, "Chief, remember Absalom."

As you'll recall, my mother named me after King David in the Bible. Absalom was David's third son, and he'd tried to kill his father. As he conspired to take his dad's life, he eventually lost his own: Some of the men in David's army killed Absalom. David was as flawed as we all are, but he loved God, and the Lord granted favor to him—the Scripture refers to David as a man after God's own heart. Still, David bore the burden of losing his child under circumstances not altogether different from the ones in which I'd lost D.J. That became my comfort. God never promised that even His most faithful servants would live free of heartache. He only promises that, when the inevitable hardships occur, He will grant us the grace to handle them. I'd been walking around with the belief that my efforts to stay faithful—to extend myself in a spirit of generosity to others, to attend church on Sundays rather than relaxing in front of the TV to watch football—would somehow shield me from the agonies life metes out. But none of us gets through life without sorrow; nor can we ever do enough good deeds to merit the good Lord's grace. His mercies come free of charge.

Out of my tragedy, two unexpected blessings emerged. The first was a profound and enduring sense of perspective. My son's loss kept all the political shenanigans, all the times when I was criticized for making a tough call, all the public pleas for my resignation, in their proper place—which is nowhere near the top of the list of what truly matters in life. Once you've put your child in the ground, nothing else can wound you as deeply. My greatest heartache eventually became my Kevlar shield. Yes, there were times when the challenges of the job did work me over pretty badly, but even as I walked through those times, I held strong to one of my anchors: the memory of my son's life. If D.J. or any of the people whose lives he cut short had had just one more breath, one more opportunity to have even what I considered to be my toughest day, I'm sure each would've given anything for that blessing. When I confronted the pettiness of politics, it all seemed so small in the face of losing a son. A brother. A partner.

The second unforeseen blessing that flowed from my loss was this: I became uniquely suited to pass on hope and encouragement to others. Every challenge prepares you for the next, and in my view, nothing happens by accident. Even when we cannot see the purpose in our pain, I believe such a purpose exists. The tragedy I experienced not only bolstered my faith; it also made me stronger at heart. And yet I never had to understand the point of the crisis or appreciate its outcome in order to use it as a powerful testimony, a healing balm for others who are confronting crisis. That is what the members of Southern Crest Full Gospel Baptist Church once did for me after I stumbled my way to the front of the sanctuary, weeping and ready to turn my back on everything I believed. They held me up and stood beside me in my grief—just as I have sought to stand with others. I now recognize that as part of my calling.

There is one other gift that came out of my tragedy—the gift of true and sincere expression to my loved ones who are still here with me, in the flesh. My family has always known that I love them. D.J. knew that as well. Yet in hindsight, there were so many times when I could've said those words out loud but did not. I thought the people closest to me would just sense my love, that they'd see all the hours I put in on the job providing for them as evidence of my deep care for them. But they could not read my mind, and even though they could see the sacrifices I was making, they still needed to hear me express love. Life and loss have taught me not to take my family for granted, and these days I'm telling them more frequently just how much they mean to me. It's easy to think, *Oh, I'll say that later,* or to assume I don't have to say it at all. But tomorrow or even the very next breath is not certain for any of us. I can't change what I did yesterday or last month or twenty years ago, but I can step up now and reveal what has always been in my heart.

Passionate leadership comes with a high cost: time away from family. When I look back over my life, I do wish I'd spent more time with my loved ones, even as the call to service and the long hours on the force consumed me. And while I carved out time in every way I could, the graveyard shifts I worked and the moonlighting jobs I took meant that I missed out on far too many day-to-day family moments and memories. But neither you nor I can get that time back. All we can do is look ahead and redeem today as a chance to be present for those closest to us. To show up for them in ways that we haven't before. To hug them more tightly than we ever have.

———

I'M STILL WRITING THE NEXT CHAPTER of my story. Even now, in retirement, I'm as ambitious as I've always been—only I'm driven by different forces than the ones that first compelled me to enter the police academy.

As much as I know God's unmerited favor was freely given, I still feel as if I owe something—that I have a debt to repay in the form of service. I'm still sorting out all the various forms that service will take, and to whom I will offer it. But that desire to give back has made me restless. It's why I can't just retire and go play golf. At so many points along my path, things could have gone so differently. I could have been born into a different family, one that did not create for me the foundation of strength and faith that my mother and great-grandmother Mabel provided. As a junior high school kid in San Francisco, the half puff I took of that cigarette could have set me up to experiment with the crack cocaine that later turned Oak Cliff into a hellhole. When I was bused to a school where the other students disdained me, God sent one blond classmate to show me kindness in a place of cruelty. When I was in SWAT, there were countless times when I could have leaned left instead of right, and in so doing, I would have been killed. Even the tragedies I experienced turned out in my favor. And from those to whom much has been given, much is required.

As a way to give back, I joined multiple boards. I became a senior adviser for Rainwater Charitable Foundation, which seeks to improve public education for children. I also became a board member for two other organizations: the Meadows Mental Health Policy Institute, whose leaders work to bolster mental health services and funding in Texas; and with the Dallas Mavericks professional basketball team to serve the community.

Even now I'm also exploring ways I can help our youth monetize their passions through business ownership. College is for some, but for not all. Many families in poor communities simply do not have the money to send their children to college. So many of the drug dealers I arrested were naturally business-minded; they have to keep a multimillion-dollar industry flowing smoothly year after year. Why not help the formerly incarcerated, for instance, set up legitimate small businesses in their underserved neighborhoods? Not only would this approach financially revitalize those neighborhoods; it would also give ex-offenders, who can't get work with a record, an opportunity to put their skills to good use while earning money above the table. Nearly any successful business owner will tell you that once you get a taste of entrepreneurship, you never want to work for anybody else but yourself.

In addition to business training, I want to see more resources for and encouragement of technical and trade school training programs. Not every child is academically gifted or has the grades or desire to take on higher education. Many don't even leave their parents' homes. If we can equip these students with the skills they need to find some meaningful form of work as an alternative, we can keep more of our youth off the streets—and out of jail cells.

In January 2017, I took another step in making a contribution. I joined the team at ABC News to serve as an on-air contributor, addressing all the issues I've come to care about: community policing, social justice and race relations, the relationship between the public and the officers who serve them, and economic equality. I've had my issues with how matters of policing are sometimes covered in the media—particularly when I was chief—which is why I've specifically chosen to become part of the press. It's a cop-out to complain about something if you're unwilling to become a change agent. This new role will give me an opportunity to make my voice heard—and, I hope, to initiate some kind of positive shift in our collective narrative.

When it comes to bringing our country together across racial lines, Dallas served as a template in the weeks after July 7. People gathered in prayer vigils, and in dozens of instances across the city, they came together for hard conversations about race and policing. Tragedy has a way of making us more open to one another. It breaks down walls. And in Dallas, those who'd previously been attached to their assumptions started really listening—hearing not just with their ears but with their hearts, even if it meant abandoning beliefs that fueled animosity and division.

It's not enough to just give lip service to reconciliation. We actually have to come together, face-to-face, with people who don't look like us, who don't share our viewpoints, and then search for common ground. We have to be willing to hold our own families and others in our community accountable for the words they speak behind closed doors and the beliefs they hold about people of different racial backgrounds. Race is an uncomfortable conversation for many, but now more than ever, it's one we need to have in this country. And we need voices of moderation in the public, which is why I took on a role in the media. I want to be one of those voices.

It is also one of the main reasons I wrote this book. I would not be spilling my guts on these pages if I did not think it would do some sort of good, perhaps by lending light to the complex issues our country and its police departments are facing.

It took losing my son for me to see other young people as I saw D.J.—to regard them with the same level of love, attentiveness, and care that I gave to my own son. When I wake every morning, I think, *Is what I'm going to do through my work on television or through volunteerism going to get us talking about drug use and mental illness? What can I say or do to light the way for families struggling with these issues? How am I going to leverage my platform to really help young people? How can I engage and promote the natural entrepreneurial talent of would-be drug lords in our neighborhoods? If I respond to a request to become involved in an effort, will that effort lead to greater mental health funding for a community that otherwise would not have it?* These are just some of the questions that get me out of bed every day. I will not rest until I've found some answers.

I have a part to play, and so do we all. Every one of us is called to rise: parents and police officers, pastors and PTA members, activists and ordinary citizens who simply want to bring about a change in our country. We need more teachers like the one who put me on the right path in second grade and like Miss Battle, who kept up with me from high school onward. We need mentors like the one who changed my course in twelfth grade, Judge Baraka. We all have a place, as well as a contribution to make.

Maybe, just maybe, we can bring about change in our country—if the Lord says the same and the creek don't rise, as we Southerners often say. Maybe the platform and notoriety I've been given, through my work on television, my speech making, or my community service can play a small part in bringing our

254 | CALLED TO RISE

country together, in restoring what is broken, and in healing what is wounded during these challenging times we find ourselves in. I wonder. I pray. I hope.

IN MANY WAYS, MY LIFE has brought me full circle. Not long after I retired, Southern Methodist University presented me with an award for ethical service. I was honored to receive the award, particularly since it was given in the name of J. Erik Jonsson, a former Dallas mayor, as well as the former CEO of Texas Instruments. Jonsson once made the decision to hire the first group of African-Americans at TI—including my mother, Norma Jean. The resulting pay allowed her to send my brother Rickey and me to a private Catholic school. That one investment is what set me up for academic success. I don't know if Jonsson, who passed away in 1995, was ever aware that this one choice changed the course for so many young people—for *me*.

Another full-circle moment came during my very last days on the force. One afternoon I came in and noticed my secretary, Anitra Ramos, weeping. "What's wrong?" I asked her. "You have to read this letter," she said, dabbing at her eyes and handing me an envelope. After the July 7 tragedy, letters had been pouring in. I walked over, took the envelope, immediately noticing the Texas longhorn stamp on it. I took it into my office and sat down and read it. "I don't know if you'll remember me," the letter began, "but you and I once sat next to each other on a Greyhound bus ride from Dallas to UT Austin." He went on to say how much that interaction, one I'd long since forgotten, had meant to him. In the same way that my sixth-grade connection with Mike Shillingburg had changed my perception, so, too, had Lance's racial lens shifted, simply because I'd shown him kindness and shared my meal. Such a brief encounter had had a powerful ripple effect.

The fact that my path crossed with Lance's was no more coincidental than any other encounter I've had. I believe God foresaw how every intersection on my journey would lead me exactly in the direction I was meant to travel. It may be years before I understand why my journey carried me from Oak Cliff to UT Austin to beat cop to chief of the Dallas Police Department, with plenty of challenges in between each of those milestones. I may never fully understand why I've taken that route. And yet it has never been more clear that whatever the Lord means for me to experience, can't anybody stop it.

Grace—it is the mystery that permeates my story from beginning to end. It cannot be earned; nor does it ever run dry. In fact, it often appears exactly when it's most needed, during times of great heartache and trial. And it doesn't just show up. When it arrives, it changes everything.

ACKNOWLEDGMENTS

——

TO MY TWO GIRLS—MY DARLING WIFE, CEDONIA, AND MY daughter, Ayana. I love you.

To my agents, Paul Fedorko and Neil Cohen—thank you for all of your behind-the-scenes work in bringing my story to the world. I appreciate you both.

To my coauthor, Michelle Burford—thank you for such heartfelt writing, and for guiding me through the editorial process.

To my editors, Porscha Burke and Brendan Vaughan—I'm grateful for the time and care you put into refining the narrative.

And of course, I will always be thankful to the entire team at Ballantine: Kara Welsh, Gina Centrello, Jennifer Hershey, Kim Hovey, Susan Corcoran, Michelle Jasmine, Quinn Rogers, Benjamin Dreyer, Lisa Feuer, Ted Allen, Mark Maguire, Paolo Pepe, Marietta Anastassatos, Barbara Bachman, Carol Poticny, Bill Takes, Sanyu Dillon, Theresa Zoro, Scott Shannon, Cynthia Lasky, and the extraordinary sales force. Your support and enthusiasm for the project have been invaluable.

PHOTOGRAPH CREDITS

A LL PHOTOS ARE REPRINTED COURTESY OF THE AUTHOR, with the exception of the following:

ABOUT THE AUTHORS

DAVID O. BROWN is a thirty-three-year veteran of the Dallas Police Department, where he retired as chief in October 2016. Chief Brown currently serves as a contributor to ABC News, and advises on several boards, including the Rainwater Charitable Foundation, Early Matters Dallas, and the Meadows Mental Health Policy Institute. He is a community relations liaison with the Dallas Mavericks and co-chair of Law Enforcement Leaders to Reduce Crime and Incarceration. His focus in these endeavors is to influence early childhood education efforts, mental health awareness and treatment, and assistance for formerly incarcerated persons. Chief Brown resides in Dallas with his wife and daughter. This is his first book.

Twitter: @ChiefDavidBrown

MICHELLE BURFORD is a #1 *New York Times* bestselling author and a founding editor of *O: The Oprah Magazine*. She is a Harvard-trained journalist whose work has taken her to more than thirty-five countries on six continents. A native of Phoenix, Burford now resides in New York City.

MichelleBurford.com